TWELFTH NIGHT

by
William Shakespeare

TABLE OF CONTENTS

Act I

SCENE I.

DUKE ORSINO's palace...5

SCENE II.

The sea-coast...6

SCENE III.

OLIVIA'S house...9

SCENE IV.

DUKE ORSINO's palace...14

SCENE V.

OLIVIA'S house..15

Act II

SCENE I.

The sea-coast...27

SCENE II.

A street..28

SCENE III.

OLIVIA's house..30

SCENE IV.

DUKE ORSINO's palace...37

SCENE V.

OLIVIA's garden..41

Act III

SCENE I.

    OLIVIA's garden. 49

SCENE II.

    OLIVIA's house. 55

SCENE III.

    A street. 58

SCENE IV.

    OLIVIA's garden. 60

Act IV

SCENE I.

    Before OLIVIA's house. 74

SCENE II.

    OLIVIA's house. 76

SCENE III.

    OLIVIA's garden. 81

Act V

SCENE I.

    Before OLIVIA's house. 83

Act I

SCENE I.

DUKE ORSINO's palace.

Enter DUKE ORSINO, CURIO, and other Lords; Musicians attending

DUKE ORSINO
If music be the food of love, play on;
Give me excess of it, that, surfeiting,
The appetite may sicken, and so die.
That strain again! it had a dying fall:
O, it came o'er my ear like the sweet sound,
That breathes upon a bank of violets,
Stealing and giving odour! Enough; no more:
'Tis not so sweet now as it was before.
O spirit of love! how quick and fresh art thou,
That, notwithstanding thy capacity
Receiveth as the sea, nought enters there,
Of what validity and pitch soe'er,
But falls into abatement and low price,
Even in a minute: so full of shapes is fancy
That it alone is high fantastical.
CURIO
Will you go hunt, my lord?
DUKE ORSINO
What, Curio?
CURIO
The hart.
DUKE ORSINO
Why, so I do, the noblest that I have:
O, when mine eyes did see Olivia first,
Methought she purged the air of pestilence!

That instant was I turn'd into a hart;
And my desires, like fell and cruel hounds,
E'er since pursue me.
Enter VALENTINE
How now! what news from her?
VALENTINE
So please my lord, I might not be admitted;
But from her handmaid do return this answer:
The element itself, till seven years' heat,
Shall not behold her face at ample view;
But, like a cloistress, she will veiled walk
And water once a day her chamber round
With eye-offending brine: all this to season
A brother's dead love, which she would keep fresh
And lasting in her sad remembrance.
DUKE ORSINO
O, she that hath a heart of that fine frame
To pay this debt of love but to a brother,
How will she love, when the rich golden shaft
Hath kill'd the flock of all affections else
That live in her; when liver, brain and heart,
These sovereign thrones, are all supplied, and fill'd
Her sweet perfections with one self king!
Away before me to sweet beds of flowers:
Love-thoughts lie rich when canopied with bowers.
Exeunt

SCENE II.

The sea-coast.

Enter VIOLA, a Captain, and Sailors
VIOLA
What country, friends, is this?
Captain
This is Illyria, lady.
VIOLA
And what should I do in Illyria?
My brother he is in Elysium.

Perchance he is not drown'd: what think you, sailors?
Captain
It is perchance that you yourself were saved.
VIOLA
O my poor brother! and so perchance may he be.
Captain
True, madam: and, to comfort you with chance,
Assure yourself, after our ship did split,
When you and those poor number saved with you
Hung on our driving boat, I saw your brother,
Most provident in peril, bind himself,
Courage and hope both teaching him the practise,
To a strong mast that lived upon the sea;
Where, like Arion on the dolphin's back,
I saw him hold acquaintance with the waves
So long as I could see.
VIOLA
For saying so, there's gold:
Mine own escape unfoldeth to my hope,
Whereto thy speech serves for authority,
The like of him. Know'st thou this country?
Captain
Ay, madam, well; for I was bred and born
Not three hours' travel from this very place.
VIOLA
Who governs here?
Captain
A noble duke, in nature as in name.
VIOLA
What is the name?
Captain
Orsino.
VIOLA
Orsino! I have heard my father name him:
He was a bachelor then.
Captain
And so is now, or was so very late;
For but a month ago I went from hence,
And then 'twas fresh in murmur,—as, you know,
What great ones do the less will prattle of,—
That he did seek the love of fair Olivia.

VIOLA
What's she?
Captain
A virtuous maid, the daughter of a count
That died some twelvemonth since, then leaving her
In the protection of his son, her brother,
Who shortly also died: for whose dear love,
They say, she hath abjured the company
And sight of men.
VIOLA
O that I served that lady
And might not be delivered to the world,
Till I had made mine own occasion mellow,
What my estate is!
Captain
That were hard to compass;
Because she will admit no kind of suit,
No, not the duke's.
VIOLA
There is a fair behavior in thee, captain;
And though that nature with a beauteous wall
Doth oft close in pollution, yet of thee
I will believe thou hast a mind that suits
With this thy fair and outward character.
I prithee, and I'll pay thee bounteously,
Conceal me what I am, and be my aid
For such disguise as haply shall become
The form of my intent. I'll serve this duke:
Thou shall present me as an eunuch to him:
It may be worth thy pains; for I can sing
And speak to him in many sorts of music
That will allow me very worth his service.
What else may hap to time I will commit;
Only shape thou thy silence to my wit.
Captain
Be you his eunuch, and your mute I'll be:
When my tongue blabs, then let mine eyes not see.
VIOLA
I thank thee: lead me on.
Exeunt

SCENE III.

OLIVIA'S house.

Enter SIR TOBY BELCH and MARIA

SIR TOBY BELCH

What a plague means my niece, to take the death of
her brother thus? I am sure care's an enemy to life.

MARIA

By my troth, Sir Toby, you must come in earlier o'
nights: your cousin, my lady, takes great
exceptions to your ill hours.

SIR TOBY BELCH

Why, let her except, before excepted.

MARIA

Ay, but you must confine yourself within the modest
limits of order.

SIR TOBY BELCH

Confine! I'll confine myself no finer than I am:
these clothes are good enough to drink in; and so be
these boots too: an they be not, let them hang
themselves in their own straps.

MARIA

That quaffing and drinking will undo you: I heard
my lady talk of it yesterday; and of a foolish
knight that you brought in one night here to be her wooer.

SIR TOBY BELCH

Who, Sir Andrew Aguecheek?

MARIA

Ay, he.

SIR TOBY BELCH

He's as tall a man as any's in Illyria.

MARIA

What's that to the purpose?

SIR TOBY BELCH

Why, he has three thousand ducats a year.

MARIA

Ay, but he'll have but a year in all these ducats:
he's a very fool and a prodigal.

SIR TOBY BELCH

Fie, that you'll say so! he plays o' the
viol-de-gamboys, and speaks three or four languages
word for word without book, and hath all the good
gifts of nature.

MARIA

He hath indeed, almost natural: for besides that
he's a fool, he's a great quarreller: and but that
he hath the gift of a coward to allay the gust he
hath in quarrelling, 'tis thought among the prudent
he would quickly have the gift of a grave.

SIR TOBY BELCH

By this hand, they are scoundrels and subtractors
that say so of him. Who are they?

MARIA

They that add, moreover, he's drunk nightly in your company.

SIR TOBY BELCH

With drinking healths to my niece: I'll drink to
her as long as there is a passage in my throat and
drink in Illyria: he's a coward and a coystrill
that will not drink to my niece till his brains turn
o' the toe like a parish-top. What, wench!
Castiliano vulgo! for here comes Sir Andrew Agueface.

Enter SIR ANDREW

SIR ANDREW

Sir Toby Belch! how now, Sir Toby Belch!

SIR TOBY BELCH

Sweet Sir Andrew!

SIR ANDREW

Bless you, fair shrew.

MARIA

And you too, sir.

SIR TOBY BELCH

Accost, Sir Andrew, accost.

SIR ANDREW

What's that?

SIR TOBY BELCH

My niece's chambermaid.

SIR ANDREW

Good Mistress Accost, I desire better acquaintance.

MARIA
My name is Mary, sir.
SIR ANDREW
Good Mistress Mary Accost,—
SIR TOBY BELCH
You mistake, knight; 'accost' is front her, board
her, woo her, assail her.
SIR ANDREW
By my troth, I would not undertake her in this
company. Is that the meaning of 'accost'?
MARIA
Fare you well, gentlemen.
SIR TOBY BELCH
An thou let part so, Sir Andrew, would thou mightst
never draw sword again.
SIR ANDREW
An you part so, mistress, I would I might never
draw sword again. Fair lady, do you think you have
fools in hand?
MARIA
Sir, I have not you by the hand.
SIR ANDREW
Marry, but you shall have; and here's my hand.
MARIA
Now, sir, 'thought is free:' I pray you, bring
your hand to the buttery-bar and let it drink.
SIR ANDREW
Wherefore, sweet-heart? what's your metaphor?
MARIA
It's dry, sir.
SIR ANDREW
Why, I think so: I am not such an ass but I can
keep my hand dry. But what's your jest?
MARIA
A dry jest, sir.
SIR ANDREW
Are you full of them?
MARIA
Ay, sir, I have them at my fingers' ends: marry,
now I let go your hand, I am barren.
Exit

SIR TOBY BELCH

O knight thou lackest a cup of canary: when did I
see thee so put down?

SIR ANDREW

Never in your life, I think; unless you see canary
put me down. Methinks sometimes I have no more wit
than a Christian or an ordinary man has: but I am a
great eater of beef and I believe that does harm to my wit.

SIR TOBY BELCH

No question.

SIR ANDREW

An I thought that, I'ld forswear it. I'll ride home
to-morrow, Sir Toby.

SIR TOBY BELCH

Pourquoi, my dear knight?

SIR ANDREW

What is 'Pourquoi'? do or not do? I would I had
bestowed that time in the tongues that I have in
fencing, dancing and bear-baiting: O, had I but
followed the arts!

SIR TOBY BELCH

Then hadst thou had an excellent head of hair.

SIR ANDREW

Why, would that have mended my hair?

SIR TOBY BELCH

Past question; for thou seest it will not curl by nature.

SIR ANDREW

But it becomes me well enough, does't not?

SIR TOBY BELCH

Excellent; it hangs like flax on a distaff; and I
hope to see a housewife take thee between her legs
and spin it off.

SIR ANDREW

Faith, I'll home to-morrow, Sir Toby: your niece
will not be seen; or if she be, it's four to one
she'll none of me: the count himself here hard by woos her.

SIR TOBY BELCH

She'll none o' the count: she'll not match above
her degree, neither in estate, years, nor wit; I
have heard her swear't. Tut, there's life in't,
man.

SIR ANDREW
I'll stay a month longer. I am a fellow o' the
strangest mind i' the world; I delight in masques
and revels sometimes altogether.

SIR TOBY BELCH
Art thou good at these kickshawses, knight?

SIR ANDREW
As any man in Illyria, whatsoever he be, under the
degree of my betters; and yet I will not compare
with an old man.

SIR TOBY BELCH
What is thy excellence in a galliard, knight?

SIR ANDREW
Faith, I can cut a caper.

SIR TOBY BELCH
And I can cut the mutton to't.

SIR ANDREW
And I think I have the back-trick simply as strong
as any man in Illyria.

SIR TOBY BELCH
Wherefore are these things hid? wherefore have
these gifts a curtain before 'em? are they like to
take dust, like Mistress Mall's picture? why dost
thou not go to church in a galliard and come home in
a coranto? My very walk should be a jig; I would not
so much as make water but in a sink-a-pace. What
dost thou mean? Is it a world to hide virtues in?
I did think, by the excellent constitution of thy
leg, it was formed under the star of a galliard.

SIR ANDREW
Ay, 'tis strong, and it does indifferent well in a
flame-coloured stock. Shall we set about some revels?

SIR TOBY BELCH
What shall we do else? were we not born under Taurus?

SIR ANDREW
Taurus! That's sides and heart.

SIR TOBY BELCH
No, sir; it is legs and thighs. Let me see the
caper; ha! higher: ha, ha! excellent!
Exeunt

SCENE IV.

DUKE ORSINO's palace.

Enter VALENTINE and VIOLA in man's attire
VALENTINE
If the duke continue these favours towards you,
Cesario, you are like to be much advanced: he hath
known you but three days, and already you are no stranger.
VIOLA
You either fear his humour or my negligence, that
you call in question the continuance of his love:
is he inconstant, sir, in his favours?
VALENTINE
No, believe me.
VIOLA
I thank you. Here comes the count.
Enter DUKE ORSINO, CURIO, and Attendants
DUKE ORSINO
Who saw Cesario, ho?
VIOLA
On your attendance, my lord; here.
DUKE ORSINO
Stand you a while aloof, Cesario,
Thou know'st no less but all; I have unclasp'd
To thee the book even of my secret soul:
Therefore, good youth, address thy gait unto her;
Be not denied access, stand at her doors,
And tell them, there thy fixed foot shall grow
Till thou have audience.
VIOLA
Sure, my noble lord,
If she be so abandon'd to her sorrow
As it is spoke, she never will admit me.
DUKE ORSINO
Be clamorous and leap all civil bounds
Rather than make unprofited return.
VIOLA
Say I do speak with her, my lord, what then?

DUKE ORSINO
O, then unfold the passion of my love,
Surprise her with discourse of my dear faith:
It shall become thee well to act my woes;
She will attend it better in thy youth
Than in a nuncio's of more grave aspect.
VIOLA
I think not so, my lord.
DUKE ORSINO
Dear lad, believe it;
For they shall yet belie thy happy years,
That say thou art a man: Diana's lip
Is not more smooth and rubious; thy small pipe
Is as the maiden's organ, shrill and sound,
And all is semblative a woman's part.
I know thy constellation is right apt
For this affair. Some four or five attend him;
All, if you will; for I myself am best
When least in company. Prosper well in this,
And thou shalt live as freely as thy lord,
To call his fortunes thine.
VIOLA
I'll do my best
To woo your lady:
Aside
yet, a barful strife!
Whoe'er I woo, myself would be his wife.
Exeunt

SCENE V.

OLIVIA'S house.

Enter MARIA and Clown
MARIA
Nay, either tell me where thou hast been, or I will
not open my lips so wide as a bristle may enter in
way of thy excuse: my lady will hang thee for thy absence.

Clown

Let her hang me: he that is well hanged in this
world needs to fear no colours.

MARIA

Make that good.

Clown

He shall see none to fear.

MARIA

A good lenten answer: I can tell thee where that
saying was born, of 'I fear no colours.'

Clown

Where, good Mistress Mary?

MARIA

In the wars; and that may you be bold to say in your foolery.

Clown

Well, God give them wisdom that have it; and those
that are fools, let them use their talents.

MARIA

Yet you will be hanged for being so long absent; or,
to be turned away, is not that as good as a hanging to you?

Clown

Many a good hanging prevents a bad marriage; and,
for turning away, let summer bear it out.

MARIA

You are resolute, then?

Clown

Not so, neither; but I am resolved on two points.

MARIA

That if one break, the other will hold; or, if both
break, your gaskins fall.

Clown

Apt, in good faith; very apt. Well, go thy way; if
Sir Toby would leave drinking, thou wert as witty a
piece of Eve's flesh as any in Illyria.

MARIA

Peace, you rogue, no more o' that. Here comes my
lady: make your excuse wisely, you were best.
Exit

Clown

Wit, an't be thy will, put me into good fooling!
Those wits, that think they have thee, do very oft

prove fools; and I, that am sure I lack thee, may
pass for a wise man: for what says Quinapalus?
'Better a witty fool, than a foolish wit.'
Enter OLIVIA with MALVOLIO
God bless thee, lady!

OLIVIA

Take the fool away.

Clown

Do you not hear, fellows? Take away the lady.

OLIVIA

Go to, you're a dry fool; I'll no more of you:
besides, you grow dishonest.

Clown

Two faults, madonna, that drink and good counsel
will amend: for give the dry fool drink, then is
the fool not dry: bid the dishonest man mend
himself; if he mend, he is no longer dishonest; if
he cannot, let the botcher mend him. Any thing
that's mended is but patched: virtue that
transgresses is but patched with sin; and sin that
amends is but patched with virtue. If that this
simple syllogism will serve, so; if it will not,
what remedy? As there is no true cuckold but
calamity, so beauty's a flower. The lady bade take
away the fool; therefore, I say again, take her away.

OLIVIA

Sir, I bade them take away you.

Clown

Misprision in the highest degree! Lady, cucullus non
facit monachum; that's as much to say as I wear not
motley in my brain. Good madonna, give me leave to
prove you a fool.

OLIVIA

Can you do it?

Clown

Dexterously, good madonna.

OLIVIA

Make your proof.

Clown

I must catechise you for it, madonna: good my mouse
of virtue, answer me.

OLIVIA

Well, sir, for want of other idleness, I'll bide your proof.

Clown

Good madonna, why mournest thou?

OLIVIA

Good fool, for my brother's death.

Clown

I think his soul is in hell, madonna.

OLIVIA

I know his soul is in heaven, fool.

Clown

The more fool, madonna, to mourn for your brother's
soul being in heaven. Take away the fool, gentlemen.

OLIVIA

What think you of this fool, Malvolio? doth he not mend?

MALVOLIO

Yes, and shall do till the pangs of death shake him:
infirmity, that decays the wise, doth ever make the
better fool.

Clown

God send you, sir, a speedy infirmity, for the
better increasing your folly! Sir Toby will be
sworn that I am no fox; but he will not pass his
word for two pence that you are no fool.

OLIVIA

How say you to that, Malvolio?

MALVOLIO

I marvel your ladyship takes delight in such a
barren rascal: I saw him put down the other day
with an ordinary fool that has no more brain
than a stone. Look you now, he's out of his guard
already; unless you laugh and minister occasion to
him, he is gagged. I protest, I take these wise men,
that crow so at these set kind of fools, no better
than the fools' zanies.

OLIVIA

Oh, you are sick of self-love, Malvolio, and taste
with a distempered appetite. To be generous,
guiltless and of free disposition, is to take those
things for bird-bolts that you deem cannon-bullets:
there is no slander in an allowed fool, though he do

nothing but rail; nor no railing in a known discreet
man, though he do nothing but reprove.

Clown

Now Mercury endue thee with leasing, for thou
speakest well of fools!

Re-enter MARIA

MARIA

Madam, there is at the gate a young gentleman much
desires to speak with you.

OLIVIA

From the Count Orsino, is it?

MARIA

I know not, madam: 'tis a fair young man, and well attended.

OLIVIA

Who of my people hold him in delay?

MARIA

Sir Toby, madam, your kinsman.

OLIVIA

Fetch him off, I pray you; he speaks nothing but
madman: fie on him!

Exit MARIA

Go you, Malvolio: if it be a suit from the count, I
am sick, or not at home; what you will, to dismiss it.

Exit MALVOLIO

Now you see, sir, how your fooling grows old, and
people dislike it.

Clown

Thou hast spoke for us, madonna, as if thy eldest
son should be a fool; whose skull Jove cram with
brains! for,—here he comes,—one of thy kin has a
most weak pia mater.

Enter SIR TOBY BELCH

OLIVIA

By mine honour, half drunk. What is he at the gate, cousin?

SIR TOBY BELCH

A gentleman.

OLIVIA

A gentleman! what gentleman?

SIR TOBY BELCH

'Tis a gentle man here—a plague o' these
pickle-herring! How now, sot!

Clown

Good Sir Toby!

OLIVIA

Cousin, cousin, how have you come so early by this lethargy?

SIR TOBY BELCH

Lechery! I defy lechery. There's one at the gate.

OLIVIA

Ay, marry, what is he?

SIR TOBY BELCH

Let him be the devil, an he will, I care not: give
me faith, say I. Well, it's all one.

Exit

OLIVIA

What's a drunken man like, fool?

Clown

Like a drowned man, a fool and a mad man: one
draught above heat makes him a fool; the second mads
him; and a third drowns him.

OLIVIA

Go thou and seek the crowner, and let him sit o' my
coz; for he's in the third degree of drink, he's
drowned: go, look after him.

Clown

He is but mad yet, madonna; and the fool shall look
to the madman.

Exit

Re-enter MALVOLIO

MALVOLIO

Madam, yond young fellow swears he will speak with
you. I told him you were sick; he takes on him to
understand so much, and therefore comes to speak
with you. I told him you were asleep; he seems to
have a foreknowledge of that too, and therefore
comes to speak with you. What is to be said to him,
lady? he's fortified against any denial.

OLIVIA

Tell him he shall not speak with me.

MALVOLIO

Has been told so; and he says, he'll stand at your
door like a sheriff's post, and be the supporter to
a bench, but he'll speak with you.

OLIVIA

What kind o' man is he?

MALVOLIO

Why, of mankind.

OLIVIA

What manner of man?

MALVOLIO

Of very ill manner; he'll speak with you, will you or no.

OLIVIA

Of what personage and years is he?

MALVOLIO

Not yet old enough for a man, nor young enough for
a boy; as a squash is before 'tis a peascod, or a
cooling when 'tis almost an apple: 'tis with him
in standing water, between boy and man. He is very
well-favoured and he speaks very shrewishly; one
would think his mother's milk were scarce out of him.

OLIVIA

Let him approach: call in my gentlewoman.

MALVOLIO

Gentlewoman, my lady calls.

Exit

Re-enter MARIA

OLIVIA

Give me my veil: come, throw it o'er my face.
We'll once more hear Orsino's embassy.

Enter VIOLA, and Attendants

VIOLA

The honourable lady of the house, which is she?

OLIVIA

Speak to me; I shall answer for her.
Your will?

VIOLA

Most radiant, exquisite and unmatchable beauty,—I
pray you, tell me if this be the lady of the house,
for I never saw her: I would be loath to cast away
my speech, for besides that it is excellently well
penned, I have taken great pains to con it. Good
beauties, let me sustain no scorn; I am very
comptible, even to the least sinister usage.

OLIVIA

Whence came you, sir?

VIOLA

I can say little more than I have studied, and that
question's out of my part. Good gentle one, give me
modest assurance if you be the lady of the house,
that I may proceed in my speech.

OLIVIA

Are you a comedian?

VIOLA

No, my profound heart: and yet, by the very fangs
of malice I swear, I am not that I play. Are you
the lady of the house?

OLIVIA

If I do not usurp myself, I am.

VIOLA

Most certain, if you are she, you do usurp
yourself; for what is yours to bestow is not yours
to reserve. But this is from my commission: I will
on with my speech in your praise, and then show you
the heart of my message.

OLIVIA

Come to what is important in't: I forgive you the praise.

VIOLA

Alas, I took great pains to study it, and 'tis poetical.

OLIVIA

It is the more like to be feigned: I pray you,
keep it in. I heard you were saucy at my gates,
and allowed your approach rather to wonder at you
than to hear you. If you be not mad, be gone; if
you have reason, be brief: 'tis not that time of
moon with me to make one in so skipping a dialogue.

MARIA

Will you hoist sail, sir? here lies your way.

VIOLA

No, good swabber; I am to hull here a little
longer. Some mollification for your giant, sweet
lady. Tell me your mind: I am a messenger.

OLIVIA

Sure, you have some hideous matter to deliver, when
the courtesy of it is so fearful. Speak your office.

VIOLA

It alone concerns your ear. I bring no overture of
war, no taxation of homage: I hold the olive in my
hand; my words are as fun of peace as matter.

OLIVIA

Yet you began rudely. What are you? what would you?

VIOLA

The rudeness that hath appeared in me have I
learned from my entertainment. What I am, and what I
would, are as secret as maidenhead; to your ears,
divinity, to any other's, profanation.

OLIVIA

Give us the place alone: we will hear this divinity.
Exeunt MARIA and Attendants
Now, sir, what is your text?

VIOLA

Most sweet lady,—

OLIVIA

A comfortable doctrine, and much may be said of it.
Where lies your text?

VIOLA

In Orsino's bosom.

OLIVIA

In his bosom! In what chapter of his bosom?

VIOLA

To answer by the method, in the first of his heart.

OLIVIA

O, I have read it: it is heresy. Have you no more to say?

VIOLA

Good madam, let me see your face.

OLIVIA

Have you any commission from your lord to negotiate
with my face? You are now out of your text: but
we will draw the curtain and show you the picture.
Look you, sir, such a one I was this present: is't
not well done?
Unveiling

VIOLA

Excellently done, if God did all.

OLIVIA

'Tis in grain, sir; 'twill endure wind and weather.

VIOLA

'Tis beauty truly blent, whose red and white
Nature's own sweet and cunning hand laid on:
Lady, you are the cruell'st she alive,
If you will lead these graces to the grave
And leave the world no copy.

OLIVIA

O, sir, I will not be so hard-hearted; I will give
out divers schedules of my beauty: it shall be
inventoried, and every particle and utensil
labelled to my will: as, item, two lips,
indifferent red; item, two grey eyes, with lids to
them; item, one neck, one chin, and so forth. Were
you sent hither to praise me?

VIOLA

I see you what you are, you are too proud;
But, if you were the devil, you are fair.
My lord and master loves you: O, such love
Could be but recompensed, though you were crown'd
The nonpareil of beauty!

OLIVIA

How does he love me?

VIOLA

With adorations, fertile tears,
With groans that thunder love, with sighs of fire.

OLIVIA

Your lord does know my mind; I cannot love him:
Yet I suppose him virtuous, know him noble,
Of great estate, of fresh and stainless youth;
In voices well divulged, free, learn'd and valiant;
And in dimension and the shape of nature
A gracious person: but yet I cannot love him;
He might have took his answer long ago.

VIOLA

If I did love you in my master's flame,
With such a suffering, such a deadly life,
In your denial I would find no sense;
I would not understand it.

OLIVIA

Why, what would you?

VIOLA

Make me a willow cabin at your gate,
And call upon my soul within the house;
Write loyal cantons of contemned love
And sing them loud even in the dead of night;
Halloo your name to the reverberate hills
And make the babbling gossip of the air
Cry out 'Olivia!' O, You should not rest
Between the elements of air and earth,
But you should pity me!

OLIVIA

You might do much.
What is your parentage?

VIOLA

Above my fortunes, yet my state is well:
I am a gentleman.

OLIVIA

Get you to your lord;
I cannot love him: let him send no more;
Unless, perchance, you come to me again,
To tell me how he takes it. Fare you well:
I thank you for your pains: spend this for me.

VIOLA

I am no fee'd post, lady; keep your purse:
My master, not myself, lacks recompense.
Love make his heart of flint that you shall love;
And let your fervor, like my master's, be
Placed in contempt! Farewell, fair cruelty.

Exit

OLIVIA

'What is your parentage?'
'Above my fortunes, yet my state is well:
I am a gentleman.' I'll be sworn thou art;
Thy tongue, thy face, thy limbs, actions and spirit,
Do give thee five-fold blazon: not too fast:
soft, soft!
Unless the master were the man. How now!
Even so quickly may one catch the plague?
Methinks I feel this youth's perfections
With an invisible and subtle stealth
To creep in at mine eyes. Well, let it be.

What ho, Malvolio!

Re-enter MALVOLIO

MALVOLIO

Here, madam, at your service.

OLIVIA

Run after that same peevish messenger,
The county's man: he left this ring behind him,
Would I or not: tell him I'll none of it.
Desire him not to flatter with his lord,
Nor hold him up with hopes; I am not for him:
If that the youth will come this way to-morrow,
I'll give him reasons for't: hie thee, Malvolio.

MALVOLIO

Madam, I will.

Exit

OLIVIA

I do I know not what, and fear to find
Mine eye too great a flatterer for my mind.
Fate, show thy force: ourselves we do not owe;
What is decreed must be, and be this so.

Exit

Act II

SCENE I.

The sea-coast.

Enter ANTONIO and SEBASTIAN

ANTONIO

Will you stay no longer? nor will you not that I go with you?

SEBASTIAN

By your patience, no. My stars shine darkly over
me: the malignancy of my fate might perhaps
distemper yours; therefore I shall crave of you your
leave that I may bear my evils alone: it were a bad
recompense for your love, to lay any of them on you.

ANTONIO: Let me yet know of you whither you are bound.

SEBASTIAN

No, sooth, sir: my determinate voyage is mere
extravagancy. But I perceive in you so excellent a
touch of modesty, that you will not extort from me
what I am willing to keep in; therefore it charges
me in manners the rather to express myself. You
must know of me then, Antonio, my name is Sebastian,
which I called Roderigo. My father was that
Sebastian of Messaline, whom I know you have heard
of. He left behind him myself and a sister, both
born in an hour: if the heavens had been pleased,
would we had so ended! but you, sir, altered that;
for some hour before you took me from the breach of
the sea was my sister drowned.

ANTONIO

Alas the day!

SEBASTIAN

A lady, sir, though it was said she much resembled

me, was yet of many accounted beautiful: but,
though I could not with such estimable wonder
overfar believe that, yet thus far I will boldly
publish her; she bore a mind that envy could not but
call fair. She is drowned already, sir, with salt
water, though I seem to drown her remembrance again with more.

ANTONIO
Pardon me, sir, your bad entertainment.

SEBASTIAN
O good Antonio, forgive me your trouble.

ANTONIO
If you will not murder me for my love, let me be
your servant.

SEBASTIAN
If you will not undo what you have done, that is,
kill him whom you have recovered, desire it not.
Fare ye well at once: my bosom is full of kindness,
and I am yet so near the manners of my mother, that
upon the least occasion more mine eyes will tell
tales of me. I am bound to the Count Orsino's court: farewell.
Exit

ANTONIO
The gentleness of all the gods go with thee!
I have many enemies in Orsino's court,
Else would I very shortly see thee there.
But, come what may, I do adore thee so,
That danger shall seem sport, and I will go.
Exit

SCENE II.

A street.

Enter VIOLA, MALVOLIO following
MALVOLIO
Were not you even now with the Countess Olivia?

VIOLA
Even now, sir; on a moderate pace I have since
arrived but hither.

MALVOLIO

She returns this ring to you, sir: you might have
saved me my pains, to have taken it away yourself.
She adds, moreover, that you should put your lord
into a desperate assurance she will none of him:
and one thing more, that you be never so hardy to
come again in his affairs, unless it be to report
your lord's taking of this. Receive it so.

VIOLA

She took the ring of me: I'll none of it.

MALVOLIO

Come, sir, you peevishly threw it to her; and her
will is, it should be so returned: if it be worth
stooping for, there it lies in your eye; if not, be
it his that finds it.

Exit

VIOLA

I left no ring with her: what means this lady?
Fortune forbid my outside have not charm'd her!
She made good view of me; indeed, so much,
That sure methought her eyes had lost her tongue,
For she did speak in starts distractedly.
She loves me, sure; the cunning of her passion
Invites me in this churlish messenger.
None of my lord's ring! why, he sent her none.
I am the man: if it be so, as 'tis,
Poor lady, she were better love a dream.
Disguise, I see, thou art a wickedness,
Wherein the pregnant enemy does much.
How easy is it for the proper-false
In women's waxen hearts to set their forms!
Alas, our frailty is the cause, not we!
For such as we are made of, such we be.
How will this fadge? my master loves her dearly;
And I, poor monster, fond as much on him;
And she, mistaken, seems to dote on me.
What will become of this? As I am man,
My state is desperate for my master's love;
As I am woman,—now alas the day!—
What thriftless sighs shall poor Olivia breathe!
O time! thou must untangle this, not I;

It is too hard a knot for me to untie!
Exit

SCENE III.

OLIVIA's house.

Enter SIR TOBY BELCH and SIR ANDREW

SIR TOBY BELCH

Approach, Sir Andrew: not to be abed after
midnight is to be up betimes; and 'diluculo
surgere,' thou know'st,—

SIR ANDREW

Nay, my troth, I know not: but I know, to be up
late is to be up late.

SIR TOBY BELCH

A false conclusion: I hate it as an unfilled can.
To be up after midnight and to go to bed then, is
early: so that to go to bed after midnight is to go
to bed betimes. Does not our life consist of the
four elements?

SIR ANDREW

Faith, so they say; but I think it rather consists
of eating and drinking.

SIR TOBY BELCH

Thou'rt a scholar; let us therefore eat and drink.
Marian, I say! a stoup of wine!

Enter Clown

SIR ANDREW

Here comes the fool, i' faith.

Clown

How now, my hearts! did you never see the picture
of 'we three'?

SIR TOBY BELCH

Welcome, ass. Now let's have a catch.

SIR ANDREW

By my troth, the fool has an excellent breast. I
had rather than forty shillings I had such a leg,
and so sweet a breath to sing, as the fool has. In

sooth, thou wast in very gracious fooling last
night, when thou spokest of Pigrogromitus, of the
Vapians passing the equinoctial of Queubus: 'twas
very good, i' faith. I sent thee sixpence for thy
leman: hadst it?

Clown

I did impeticos thy gratillity; for Malvolio's nose
is no whipstock: my lady has a white hand, and the
Myrmidons are no bottle-ale houses.

SIR ANDREW

Excellent! why, this is the best fooling, when all
is done. Now, a song.

SIR TOBY BELCH

Come on; there is sixpence for you: let's have a song.

SIR ANDREW

There's a testril of me too: if one knight give a—

Clown

Would you have a love-song, or a song of good life?

SIR TOBY BELCH

A love-song, a love-song.

SIR ANDREW

Ay, ay: I care not for good life.

Clown

[Sings]
O mistress mine, where are you roaming?
O, stay and hear; your true love's coming,
That can sing both high and low:
Trip no further, pretty sweeting;
Journeys end in lovers meeting,
Every wise man's son doth know.

SIR ANDREW

Excellent good, i' faith.

SIR TOBY BELCH

Good, good.

Clown

[Sings]
What is love? 'tis not hereafter;
Present mirth hath present laughter;
What's to come is still unsure:
In delay there lies no plenty;
Then come kiss me, sweet and twenty,

Youth's a stuff will not endure.

SIR ANDREW

A mellifluous voice, as I am true knight.

SIR TOBY BELCH

A contagious breath.

SIR ANDREW

Very sweet and contagious, i' faith.

SIR TOBY BELCH

To hear by the nose, it is dulcet in contagion.
But shall we make the welkin dance indeed? shall we
rouse the night-owl in a catch that will draw three
souls out of one weaver? shall we do that?

SIR ANDREW

An you love me, let's do't: I am dog at a catch.

Clown

By'r lady, sir, and some dogs will catch well.

SIR ANDREW

Most certain. Let our catch be, 'Thou knave.'

Clown

'Hold thy peace, thou knave,' knight? I shall be
constrained in't to call thee knave, knight.

SIR ANDREW

'Tis not the first time I have constrained one to
call me knave. Begin, fool: it begins 'Hold thy peace.'

Clown

I shall never begin if I hold my peace.

SIR ANDREW

Good, i' faith. Come, begin.

Catch sung

Enter MARIA

MARIA

What a caterwauling do you keep here! If my lady
have not called up her steward Malvolio and bid him
turn you out of doors, never trust me.

SIR TOBY BELCH

My lady's a Cataian, we are politicians, Malvolio's
a Peg-a-Ramsey, and 'Three merry men be we.' Am not
I consanguineous? am I not of her blood?
Tillyvally. Lady!

Sings

'There dwelt a man in Babylon, lady, lady!'

Clown

Beshrew me, the knight's in admirable fooling.

SIR ANDREW

Ay, he does well enough if he be disposed, and so do
I too: he does it with a better grace, but I do it
more natural.

SIR TOBY BELCH

[Sings] 'O, the twelfth day of December,'—

MARIA

For the love o' God, peace!

Enter MALVOLIO

MALVOLIO

My masters, are you mad? or what are you? Have ye
no wit, manners, nor honesty, but to gabble like
tinkers at this time of night? Do ye make an
alehouse of my lady's house, that ye squeak out your
coziers' catches without any mitigation or remorse
of voice? Is there no respect of place, persons, nor
time in you?

SIR TOBY BELCH

We did keep time, sir, in our catches. Sneck up!

MALVOLIO

Sir Toby, I must be round with you. My lady bade me
tell you, that, though she harbours you as her
kinsman, she's nothing allied to your disorders. If
you can separate yourself and your misdemeanors, you
are welcome to the house; if not, an it would please
you to take leave of her, she is very willing to bid
you farewell.

SIR TOBY BELCH

'Farewell, dear heart, since I must needs be gone.'

MARIA

Nay, good Sir Toby.

Clown

'His eyes do show his days are almost done.'

MALVOLIO

Is't even so?

SIR TOBY BELCH

'But I will never die.'

Clown

Sir Toby, there you lie.

MALVOLIO

This is much credit to you.

SIR TOBY BELCH

'Shall I bid him go?'

Clown

'What an if you do?'

SIR TOBY BELCH

'Shall I bid him go, and spare not?'

Clown

'O no, no, no, no, you dare not.'

SIR TOBY BELCH

Out o' tune, sir: ye lie. Art any more than a
steward? Dost thou think, because thou art
virtuous, there shall be no more cakes and ale?

Clown

Yes, by Saint Anne, and ginger shall be hot i' the
mouth too.

SIR TOBY BELCH

Thou'rt i' the right. Go, sir, rub your chain with
crumbs. A stoup of wine, Maria!

MALVOLIO

Mistress Mary, if you prized my lady's favour at any
thing more than contempt, you would not give means
for this uncivil rule: she shall know of it, by this hand.

Exit

MARIA

Go shake your ears.

SIR ANDREW

'Twere as good a deed as to drink when a man's
a-hungry, to challenge him the field, and then to
break promise with him and make a fool of him.

SIR TOBY BELCH

Do't, knight: I'll write thee a challenge: or I'll
deliver thy indignation to him by word of mouth.

MARIA

Sweet Sir Toby, be patient for tonight: since the
youth of the count's was today with thy lady, she is
much out of quiet. For Monsieur Malvolio, let me
alone with him: if I do not gull him into a
nayword, and make him a common recreation, do not
think I have wit enough to lie straight in my bed:

I know I can do it.

SIR TOBY BELCH

Possess us, possess us; tell us something of him.

MARIA

Marry, sir, sometimes he is a kind of puritan.

SIR ANDREW

O, if I thought that I'ld beat him like a dog!

SIR TOBY BELCH

What, for being a puritan? thy exquisite reason,
dear knight?

SIR ANDREW

I have no exquisite reason for't, but I have reason
good enough.

MARIA

The devil a puritan that he is, or any thing
constantly, but a time-pleaser; an affectioned ass,
that cons state without book and utters it by great
swarths: the best persuaded of himself, so
crammed, as he thinks, with excellencies, that it is
his grounds of faith that all that look on him love
him; and on that vice in him will my revenge find
notable cause to work.

SIR TOBY BELCH

What wilt thou do?

MARIA

I will drop in his way some obscure epistles of
love; wherein, by the colour of his beard, the shape
of his leg, the manner of his gait, the expressure
of his eye, forehead, and complexion, he shall find
himself most feelingly personated. I can write very
like my lady your niece: on a forgotten matter we
can hardly make distinction of our hands.

SIR TOBY BELCH

Excellent! I smell a device.

SIR ANDREW

I have't in my nose too.

SIR TOBY BELCH

He shall think, by the letters that thou wilt drop,
that they come from my niece, and that she's in
love with him.

MARIA

My purpose is, indeed, a horse of that colour.

SIR ANDREW

And your horse now would make him an ass.

MARIA

Ass, I doubt not.

SIR ANDREW

O, 'twill be admirable!

MARIA

Sport royal, I warrant you: I know my physic will
work with him. I will plant you two, and let the
fool make a third, where he shall find the letter:
observe his construction of it. For this night, to
bed, and dream on the event. Farewell.

Exit

SIR TOBY BELCH

Good night, Penthesilea.

SIR ANDREW

Before me, she's a good wench.

SIR TOBY BELCH

She's a beagle, true-bred, and one that adores me:
what o' that?

SIR ANDREW

I was adored once too.

SIR TOBY BELCH

Let's to bed, knight. Thou hadst need send for
more money.

SIR ANDREW

If I cannot recover your niece, I am a foul way out.

SIR TOBY BELCH

Send for money, knight: if thou hast her not i'
the end, call me cut.

SIR ANDREW

If I do not, never trust me, take it how you will.

SIR TOBY BELCH

Come, come, I'll go burn some sack; 'tis too late
to go to bed now: come, knight; come, knight.

Exeunt

SCENE IV.

DUKE ORSINO's palace.

Enter DUKE ORSINO, VIOLA, CURIO, and others

DUKE ORSINO
Give me some music. Now, good morrow, friends.
Now, good Cesario, but that piece of song,
That old and antique song we heard last night:
Methought it did relieve my passion much,
More than light airs and recollected terms
Of these most brisk and giddy-paced times:
Come, but one verse.

CURIO
He is not here, so please your lordship that should sing it.

DUKE ORSINO
Who was it?

CURIO
Feste, the jester, my lord; a fool that the lady
Olivia's father took much delight in. He is about the house.

DUKE ORSINO
Seek him out, and play the tune the while.
Exit CURIO. Music plays
Come hither, boy: if ever thou shalt love,
In the sweet pangs of it remember me;
For such as I am all true lovers are,
Unstaid and skittish in all motions else,
Save in the constant image of the creature
That is beloved. How dost thou like this tune?

VIOLA
It gives a very echo to the seat
Where Love is throned.

DUKE ORSINO
Thou dost speak masterly:
My life upon't, young though thou art, thine eye
Hath stay'd upon some favour that it loves:
Hath it not, boy?

VIOLA
A little, by your favour.

DUKE ORSINO

What kind of woman is't?

VIOLA

Of your complexion.

DUKE ORSINO

She is not worth thee, then. What years, i' faith?

VIOLA

About your years, my lord.

DUKE ORSINO

Too old by heaven: let still the woman take
An elder than herself: so wears she to him,
So sways she level in her husband's heart:
For, boy, however we do praise ourselves,
Our fancies are more giddy and unfirm,
More longing, wavering, sooner lost and worn,
Than women's are.

VIOLA

I think it well, my lord.

DUKE ORSINO

Then let thy love be younger than thyself,
Or thy affection cannot hold the bent;
For women are as roses, whose fair flower
Being once display'd, doth fall that very hour.

VIOLA

And so they are: alas, that they are so;
To die, even when they to perfection grow!
Re-enter CURIO and Clown

DUKE ORSINO

O, fellow, come, the song we had last night.
Mark it, Cesario, it is old and plain;
The spinsters and the knitters in the sun
And the free maids that weave their thread with bones
Do use to chant it: it is silly sooth,
And dallies with the innocence of love,
Like the old age.

Clown

Are you ready, sir?

DUKE ORSINO

Ay; prithee, sing.
Music
SONG.

Clown

Come away, come away, death,
And in sad cypress let me be laid;
Fly away, fly away breath;
I am slain by a fair cruel maid.
My shroud of white, stuck all with yew,
O, prepare it!
My part of death, no one so true
Did share it.
Not a flower, not a flower sweet
On my black coffin let there be strown;
Not a friend, not a friend greet
My poor corpse, where my bones shall be thrown:
A thousand thousand sighs to save,
Lay me, O, where
Sad true lover never find my grave,
To weep there!

DUKE ORSINO

There's for thy pains.

Clown

No pains, sir: I take pleasure in singing, sir.

DUKE ORSINO

I'll pay thy pleasure then.

Clown

Truly, sir, and pleasure will be paid, one time or another.

DUKE ORSINO

Give me now leave to leave thee.

Clown

Now, the melancholy god protect thee; and the
tailor make thy doublet of changeable taffeta, for
thy mind is a very opal. I would have men of such
constancy put to sea, that their business might be
every thing and their intent every where; for that's
it that always makes a good voyage of nothing. Farewell.

Exit

DUKE ORSINO

Let all the rest give place.

CURIO and Attendants retire

Once more, Cesario,
Get thee to yond same sovereign cruelty:
Tell her, my love, more noble than the world,

Prizes not quantity of dirty lands;
The parts that fortune hath bestow'd upon her,
Tell her, I hold as giddily as fortune;
But 'tis that miracle and queen of gems
That nature pranks her in attracts my soul.

VIOLA

But if she cannot love you, sir?

DUKE ORSINO

I cannot be so answer'd.

VIOLA

Sooth, but you must.
Say that some lady, as perhaps there is,
Hath for your love a great a pang of heart
As you have for Olivia: you cannot love her;
You tell her so; must she not then be answer'd?

DUKE ORSINO

There is no woman's sides
Can bide the beating of so strong a passion
As love doth give my heart; no woman's heart
So big, to hold so much; they lack retention
Alas, their love may be call'd appetite,
No motion of the liver, but the palate,
That suffer surfeit, cloyment and revolt;
But mine is all as hungry as the sea,
And can digest as much: make no compare
Between that love a woman can bear me
And that I owe Olivia.

VIOLA

Ay, but I know—

DUKE ORSINO

What dost thou know?

VIOLA

Too well what love women to men may owe:
In faith, they are as true of heart as we.
My father had a daughter loved a man,
As it might be, perhaps, were I a woman,
I should your lordship.

DUKE ORSINO

And what's her history?

VIOLA

A blank, my lord. She never told her love,

But let concealment, like a worm i' the bud,
Feed on her damask cheek: she pined in thought,
And with a green and yellow melancholy
She sat like patience on a monument,
Smiling at grief. Was not this love indeed?
We men may say more, swear more: but indeed
Our shows are more than will; for still we prove
Much in our vows, but little in our love.

DUKE ORSINO
But died thy sister of her love, my boy?

VIOLA
I am all the daughters of my father's house,
And all the brothers too: and yet I know not.
Sir, shall I to this lady?

DUKE ORSINO
Ay, that's the theme.
To her in haste; give her this jewel; say,
My love can give no place, bide no denay.
Exeunt

SCENE V.

OLIVIA's garden.

Enter SIR TOBY BELCH, SIR ANDREW, and FABIAN
SIR TOBY BELCH
Come thy ways, Signior Fabian.

FABIAN
Nay, I'll come: if I lose a scruple of this sport,
let me be boiled to death with melancholy.

SIR TOBY BELCH
Wouldst thou not be glad to have the niggardly
rascally sheep-biter come by some notable shame?

FABIAN
I would exult, man: you know, he brought me out o'
favour with my lady about a bear-baiting here.

SIR TOBY BELCH
To anger him we'll have the bear again; and we will
fool him black and blue: shall we not, Sir Andrew?

SIR ANDREW

An we do not, it is pity of our lives.

SIR TOBY BELCH

Here comes the little villain.

Enter MARIA

How now, my metal of India!

MARIA

Get ye all three into the box-tree: Malvolio's
coming down this walk: he has been yonder i' the
sun practising behavior to his own shadow this half
hour: observe him, for the love of mockery; for I
know this letter will make a contemplative idiot of
him. Close, in the name of jesting! Lie thou there,

Throws down a letter

for here comes the trout that must be caught with tickling.

Exit

Enter MALVOLIO

MALVOLIO

'Tis but fortune; all is fortune. Maria once told
me she did affect me: and I have heard herself come
thus near, that, should she fancy, it should be one
of my complexion. Besides, she uses me with a more
exalted respect than any one else that follows her.
What should I think on't?

SIR TOBY BELCH

Here's an overweening rogue!

FABIAN

O, peace! Contemplation makes a rare turkey-cock
of him: how he jets under his advanced plumes!

SIR ANDREW

'Slight, I could so beat the rogue!

SIR TOBY BELCH

Peace, I say.

MALVOLIO

To be Count Malvolio!

SIR TOBY BELCH

Ah, rogue!

SIR ANDREW

Pistol him, pistol him.

SIR TOBY BELCH

Peace, peace!

MALVOLIO

There is example for't; the lady of the Strachy
married the yeoman of the wardrobe.

SIR ANDREW

Fie on him, Jezebel!

FABIAN

O, peace! now he's deeply in: look how
imagination blows him.

MALVOLIO

Having been three months married to her, sitting in
my state,—

SIR TOBY BELCH

O, for a stone-bow, to hit him in the eye!

MALVOLIO

Calling my officers about me, in my branched velvet
gown; having come from a day-bed, where I have left
Olivia sleeping,—

SIR TOBY BELCH

Fire and brimstone!

FABIAN

O, peace, peace!

MALVOLIO

And then to have the humour of state; and after a
demure travel of regard, telling them I know my
place as I would they should do theirs, to for my
kinsman Toby,—

SIR TOBY BELCH

Bolts and shackles!

FABIAN

O peace, peace, peace! now, now.

MALVOLIO

Seven of my people, with an obedient start, make
out for him: I frown the while; and perchance wind
up watch, or play with my—some rich jewel. Toby
approaches; courtesies there to me,—

SIR TOBY BELCH

Shall this fellow live?

FABIAN

Though our silence be drawn from us with cars, yet peace.

MALVOLIO

I extend my hand to him thus, quenching my familiar

smile with an austere regard of control,—
SIR TOBY BELCH
And does not Toby take you a blow o' the lips then?
MALVOLIO
Saying, 'Cousin Toby, my fortunes having cast me on
your niece give me this prerogative of speech,'—
SIR TOBY BELCH
What, what?
MALVOLIO
'You must amend your drunkenness.'
SIR TOBY BELCH
Out, scab!
FABIAN
Nay, patience, or we break the sinews of our plot.
MALVOLIO
'Besides, you waste the treasure of your time with
a foolish knight,'—
SIR ANDREW
That's me, I warrant you.
MALVOLIO
'One Sir Andrew,'—
SIR ANDREW
I knew 'twas I; for many do call me fool.
MALVOLIO
What employment have we here?
Taking up the letter
FABIAN
Now is the woodcock near the gin.
SIR TOBY BELCH
O, peace! and the spirit of humour intimate reading
aloud to him!
MALVOLIO
By my life, this is my lady's hand these be her
very C's, her U's and her T's and thus makes she her
great P's. It is, in contempt of question, her hand.
SIR ANDREW
Her C's, her U's and her T's: why that?
MALVOLIO
[Reads] 'To the unknown beloved, this, and my good
wishes:'—her very phrases! By your leave, wax.
Soft! and the impressure her Lucrece, with which she

uses to seal: 'tis my lady. To whom should this be?

FABIAN
This wins him, liver and all.

MALVOLIO
[Reads]
Jove knows I love: But who?
Lips, do not move;
No man must know.
'No man must know.' What follows? the numbers
altered! 'No man must know:' if this should be
thee, Malvolio?

SIR TOBY BELCH
Marry, hang thee, brock!

MALVOLIO
[Reads]
I may command where I adore;
But silence, like a Lucrece knife,
With bloodless stroke my heart doth gore:
M, O, A, I, doth sway my life.

FABIAN
A fustian riddle!

SIR TOBY BELCH
Excellent wench, say I.

MALVOLIO
'M, O, A, I, doth sway my life.' Nay, but first, let
me see, let me see, let me see.

FABIAN
What dish o' poison has she dressed him!

SIR TOBY BELCH
And with what wing the staniel cheques at it!

MALVOLIO
'I may command where I adore.' Why, she may command
me: I serve her; she is my lady. Why, this is
evident to any formal capacity; there is no
obstruction in this: and the end,—what should
that alphabetical position portend? If I could make
that resemble something in me,—Softly! M, O, A,
I,—

SIR TOBY BELCH
O, ay, make up that: he is now at a cold scent.

FABIAN

Sowter will cry upon't for all this, though it be as
rank as a fox.

MALVOLIO

M,—Malvolio; M,—why, that begins my name.

FABIAN

Did not I say he would work it out? the cur is
excellent at faults.

MALVOLIO

M,—but then there is no consonancy in the sequel;
that suffers under probation A should follow but O does.

FABIAN

And O shall end, I hope.

SIR TOBY BELCH

Ay, or I'll cudgel him, and make him cry O!

MALVOLIO

And then I comes behind.

FABIAN

Ay, an you had any eye behind you, you might see
more detraction at your heels than fortunes before
you.

MALVOLIO

M, O, A, I; this simulation is not as the former: and
yet, to crush this a little, it would bow to me, for
every one of these letters are in my name. Soft!
here follows prose.

Reads

'If this fall into thy hand, revolve. In my stars I
am above thee; but be not afraid of greatness: some
are born great, some achieve greatness, and some
have greatness thrust upon 'em. Thy Fates open
their hands; let thy blood and spirit embrace them;
and, to inure thyself to what thou art like to be,
cast thy humble slough and appear fresh. Be
opposite with a kinsman, surly with servants; let
thy tongue tang arguments of state; put thyself into
the trick of singularity: she thus advises thee
that sighs for thee. Remember who commended thy
yellow stockings, and wished to see thee ever
cross-gartered: I say, remember. Go to, thou art
made, if thou desirest to be so; if not, let me see

thee a steward still, the fellow of servants, and
not worthy to touch Fortune's fingers. Farewell.
She that would alter services with thee,
THE FORTUNATE-UNHAPPY.'
Daylight and champaign discovers not more: this is
open. I will be proud, I will read politic authors,
I will baffle Sir Toby, I will wash off gross
acquaintance, I will be point-devise the very man.
I do not now fool myself, to let imagination jade
me; for every reason excites to this, that my lady
loves me. She did commend my yellow stockings of
late, she did praise my leg being cross-gartered;
and in this she manifests herself to my love, and
with a kind of injunction drives me to these habits
of her liking. I thank my stars I am happy. I will
be strange, stout, in yellow stockings, and
cross-gartered, even with the swiftness of putting
on. Jove and my stars be praised! Here is yet a
postscript.
Reads
'Thou canst not choose but know who I am. If thou
entertainest my love, let it appear in thy smiling;
thy smiles become thee well; therefore in my
presence still smile, dear my sweet, I prithee.'
Jove, I thank thee: I will smile; I will do
everything that thou wilt have me.
Exit

FABIAN
I will not give my part of this sport for a pension
of thousands to be paid from the Sophy.

SIR TOBY BELCH
I could marry this wench for this device.

SIR ANDREW
So could I too.

SIR TOBY BELCH
And ask no other dowry with her but such another jest.

SIR ANDREW
Nor I neither.

FABIAN
Here comes my noble gull-catcher.
Re-enter MARIA

SIR TOBY BELCH

Wilt thou set thy foot o' my neck?

SIR ANDREW

Or o' mine either?

SIR TOBY BELCH

Shall I play my freedom at traytrip, and become thy bond-slave?

SIR ANDREW

I' faith, or I either?

SIR TOBY BELCH

Why, thou hast put him in such a dream, that when the image of it leaves him he must run mad.

MARIA

Nay, but say true; does it work upon him?

SIR TOBY BELCH

Like aqua-vitae with a midwife.

MARIA

If you will then see the fruits of the sport, mark his first approach before my lady: he will come to her in yellow stockings, and 'tis a colour she abhors, and cross-gartered, a fashion she detests; and he will smile upon her, which will now be so unsuitable to her disposition, being addicted to a melancholy as she is, that it cannot but turn him into a notable contempt. If you will see it, follow me.

SIR TOBY BELCH

To the gates of Tartar, thou most excellent devil of wit!

SIR ANDREW

I'll make one too.

Exeunt

Act III

SCENE I.

OLIVIA's garden.

Enter VIOLA, and Clown with a tabour

VIOLA

Save thee, friend, and thy music: dost thou live by
thy tabour?

Clown

No, sir, I live by the church.

VIOLA

Art thou a churchman?

Clown

No such matter, sir: I do live by the church; for
I do live at my house, and my house doth stand by
the church.

VIOLA

So thou mayst say, the king lies by a beggar, if a
beggar dwell near him; or, the church stands by thy
tabour, if thy tabour stand by the church.

Clown

You have said, sir. To see this age! A sentence is
but a cheveril glove to a good wit: how quickly the
wrong side may be turned outward!

VIOLA

Nay, that's certain; they that dally nicely with
words may quickly make them wanton.

Clown

I would, therefore, my sister had had no name, sir.

VIOLA

Why, man?

Clown

Why, sir, her name's a word; and to dally with that
word might make my sister wanton. But indeed words
are very rascals since bonds disgraced them.

VIOLA

Thy reason, man?

Clown

Troth, sir, I can yield you none without words; and
words are grown so false, I am loath to prove
reason with them.

VIOLA

I warrant thou art a merry fellow and carest for nothing.

Clown

Not so, sir, I do care for something; but in my
conscience, sir, I do not care for you: if that be
to care for nothing, sir, I would it would make you invisible.

VIOLA

Art not thou the Lady Olivia's fool?

Clown

No, indeed, sir; the Lady Olivia has no folly: she
will keep no fool, sir, till she be married; and
fools are as like husbands as pilchards are to
herrings; the husband's the bigger: I am indeed not
her fool, but her corrupter of words.

VIOLA

I saw thee late at the Count Orsino's.

Clown

Foolery, sir, does walk about the orb like the sun,
it shines every where. I would be sorry, sir, but
the fool should be as oft with your master as with
my mistress: I think I saw your wisdom there.

VIOLA

Nay, an thou pass upon me, I'll no more with thee.
Hold, there's expenses for thee.

Clown

Now Jove, in his next commodity of hair, send thee a beard!

VIOLA

By my troth, I'll tell thee, I am almost sick for
one;

Aside

though I would not have it grow on my chin. Is thy

lady within?

Clown

Would not a pair of these have bred, sir?

VIOLA

Yes, being kept together and put to use.

Clown

I would play Lord Pandarus of Phrygia, sir, to bring
a Cressida to this Troilus.

VIOLA

I understand you, sir; 'tis well begged.

Clown

The matter, I hope, is not great, sir, begging but
a beggar: Cressida was a beggar. My lady is
within, sir. I will construe to them whence you
come; who you are and what you would are out of my
welkin, I might say 'element,' but the word is over-worn.

Exit

VIOLA

This fellow is wise enough to play the fool;
And to do that well craves a kind of wit:
He must observe their mood on whom he jests,
The quality of persons, and the time,
And, like the haggard, cheque at every feather
That comes before his eye. This is a practise
As full of labour as a wise man's art
For folly that he wisely shows is fit;
But wise men, folly-fall'n, quite taint their wit.

Enter SIR TOBY BELCH, and SIR ANDREW

SIR TOBY BELCH

Save you, gentleman.

VIOLA

And you, sir.

SIR ANDREW

Dieu vous garde, monsieur.

VIOLA

Et vous aussi; votre serviteur.

SIR ANDREW

I hope, sir, you are; and I am yours.

SIR TOBY BELCH

Will you encounter the house? my niece is desirous
you should enter, if your trade be to her.

VIOLA

I am bound to your niece, sir; I mean, she is the
list of my voyage.

SIR TOBY BELCH

Taste your legs, sir; put them to motion.

VIOLA

My legs do better understand me, sir, than I
understand what you mean by bidding me taste my legs.

SIR TOBY BELCH

I mean, to go, sir, to enter.

VIOLA

I will answer you with gait and entrance. But we
are prevented.

Enter OLIVIA and MARIA

Most excellent accomplished lady, the heavens rain
odours on you!

SIR ANDREW

That youth's a rare courtier: 'Rain odours;' well.

VIOLA

My matter hath no voice, to your own most pregnant
and vouchsafed ear.

SIR ANDREW

'Odours,' 'pregnant' and 'vouchsafed:' I'll get 'em
all three all ready.

OLIVIA

Let the garden door be shut, and leave me to my hearing.

Exeunt SIR TOBY BELCH, SIR ANDREW, and MARIA

Give me your hand, sir.

VIOLA

My duty, madam, and most humble service.

OLIVIA

What is your name?

VIOLA

Cesario is your servant's name, fair princess.

OLIVIA

My servant, sir! 'Twas never merry world
Since lowly feigning was call'd compliment:
You're servant to the Count Orsino, youth.

VIOLA

And he is yours, and his must needs be yours:
Your servant's servant is your servant, madam.

OLIVIA

For him, I think not on him: for his thoughts,
Would they were blanks, rather than fill'd with me!

VIOLA

Madam, I come to whet your gentle thoughts
On his behalf.

OLIVIA

O, by your leave, I pray you,
I bade you never speak again of him:
But, would you undertake another suit,
I had rather hear you to solicit that
Than music from the spheres.

VIOLA

Dear lady,—

OLIVIA

Give me leave, beseech you. I did send,
After the last enchantment you did here,
A ring in chase of you: so did I abuse
Myself, my servant and, I fear me, you:
Under your hard construction must I sit,
To force that on you, in a shameful cunning,
Which you knew none of yours: what might you think?
Have you not set mine honour at the stake
And baited it with all the unmuzzled thoughts
That tyrannous heart can think? To one of your receiving
Enough is shown: a cypress, not a bosom,
Hideth my heart. So, let me hear you speak.

VIOLA

I pity you.

OLIVIA

That's a degree to love.

VIOLA

No, not a grize; for 'tis a vulgar proof,
That very oft we pity enemies.

OLIVIA

Why, then, methinks 'tis time to smile again.
O, world, how apt the poor are to be proud!
If one should be a prey, how much the better
To fall before the lion than the wolf!

Clock strikes

The clock upbraids me with the waste of time.

Be not afraid, good youth, I will not have you:
And yet, when wit and youth is come to harvest,
Your were is alike to reap a proper man:
There lies your way, due west.

VIOLA

Then westward-ho! Grace and good disposition
Attend your ladyship!
You'll nothing, madam, to my lord by me?

OLIVIA

Stay:
I prithee, tell me what thou thinkest of me.

VIOLA

That you do think you are not what you are.

OLIVIA

If I think so, I think the same of you.

VIOLA

Then think you right: I am not what I am.

OLIVIA

I would you were as I would have you be!

VIOLA

Would it be better, madam, than I am?
I wish it might, for now I am your fool.

OLIVIA

O, what a deal of scorn looks beautiful
In the contempt and anger of his lip!
A murderous guilt shows not itself more soon
Than love that would seem hid: love's night is noon.
Cesario, by the roses of the spring,
By maidhood, honour, truth and every thing,
I love thee so, that, maugre all thy pride,
Nor wit nor reason can my passion hide.
Do not extort thy reasons from this clause,
For that I woo, thou therefore hast no cause,
But rather reason thus with reason fetter,
Love sought is good, but given unsought better.

VIOLA

By innocence I swear, and by my youth
I have one heart, one bosom and one truth,
And that no woman has; nor never none
Shall mistress be of it, save I alone.
And so adieu, good madam: never more

Will I my master's tears to you deplore.
OLIVIA
Yet come again; for thou perhaps mayst move
That heart, which now abhors, to like his love.
Exeunt

SCENE II.

OLIVIA's house.

Enter SIR TOBY BELCH, SIR ANDREW, and FABIAN
SIR ANDREW
No, faith, I'll not stay a jot longer.
SIR TOBY BELCH
Thy reason, dear venom, give thy reason.
FABIAN
You must needs yield your reason, Sir Andrew.
SIR ANDREW
Marry, I saw your niece do more favours to the
count's serving-man than ever she bestowed upon me;
I saw't i' the orchard.
SIR TOBY BELCH
Did she see thee the while, old boy? tell me that.
SIR ANDREW
As plain as I see you now.
FABIAN
This was a great argument of love in her toward you.
SIR ANDREW
'Slight, will you make an ass o' me?
FABIAN
I will prove it legitimate, sir, upon the oaths of
judgment and reason.
SIR TOBY BELCH
And they have been grand-jury-men since before Noah
was a sailor.
FABIAN
She did show favour to the youth in your sight only
to exasperate you, to awake your dormouse valour, to
put fire in your heart and brimstone in your liver.

You should then have accosted her; and with some
excellent jests, fire-new from the mint, you should
have banged the youth into dumbness. This was
looked for at your hand, and this was balked: the
double gilt of this opportunity you let time wash
off, and you are now sailed into the north of my
lady's opinion; where you will hang like an icicle
on a Dutchman's beard, unless you do redeem it by
some laudable attempt either of valour or policy.

SIR ANDREW

An't be any way, it must be with valour; for policy
I hate: I had as lief be a Brownist as a
politician.

SIR TOBY BELCH

Why, then, build me thy fortunes upon the basis of
valour. Challenge me the count's youth to fight
with him; hurt him in eleven places: my niece shall
take note of it; and assure thyself, there is no
love-broker in the world can more prevail in man's
commendation with woman than report of valour.

FABIAN

There is no way but this, Sir Andrew.

SIR ANDREW

Will either of you bear me a challenge to him?

SIR TOBY BELCH

Go, write it in a martial hand; be curst and brief;
it is no matter how witty, so it be eloquent and fun
of invention: taunt him with the licence of ink:
if thou thou'st him some thrice, it shall not be
amiss; and as many lies as will lie in thy sheet of
paper, although the sheet were big enough for the
bed of Ware in England, set 'em down: go, about it.
Let there be gall enough in thy ink, though thou
write with a goose-pen, no matter: about it.

SIR ANDREW

Where shall I find you?

SIR TOBY BELCH

We'll call thee at the cubiculo: go.

Exit SIR ANDREW

FABIAN

This is a dear manikin to you, Sir Toby.

SIR TOBY BELCH
I have been dear to him, lad, some two thousand
strong, or so.

FABIAN
We shall have a rare letter from him: but you'll
not deliver't?

SIR TOBY BELCH
Never trust me, then; and by all means stir on the
youth to an answer. I think oxen and wainropes
cannot hale them together. For Andrew, if he were
opened, and you find so much blood in his liver as
will clog the foot of a flea, I'll eat the rest of
the anatomy.

FABIAN
And his opposite, the youth, bears in his visage no
great presage of cruelty.
Enter MARIA

SIR TOBY BELCH
Look, where the youngest wren of nine comes.

MARIA
If you desire the spleen, and will laugh yourself
into stitches, follow me. Yond gull Malvolio is
turned heathen, a very renegado; for there is no
Christian, that means to be saved by believing
rightly, can ever believe such impossible passages
of grossness. He's in yellow stockings.

SIR TOBY BELCH
And cross-gartered?

MARIA
Most villanously; like a pedant that keeps a school
i' the church. I have dogged him, like his
murderer. He does obey every point of the letter
that I dropped to betray him: he does smile his
face into more lines than is in the new map with the
augmentation of the Indies: you have not seen such
a thing as 'tis. I can hardly forbear hurling things
at him. I know my lady will strike him: if she do,
he'll smile and take't for a great favour.

SIR TOBY BELCH
Come, bring us, bring us where he is.
Exeunt

SCENE III.

A street.

Enter SEBASTIAN and ANTONIO
SEBASTIAN
I would not by my will have troubled you;
But, since you make your pleasure of your pains,
I will no further chide you.
ANTONIO
I could not stay behind you: my desire,
More sharp than filed steel, did spur me forth;
And not all love to see you, though so much
As might have drawn one to a longer voyage,
But jealousy what might befall your travel,
Being skilless in these parts; which to a stranger,
Unguided and unfriended, often prove
Rough and unhospitable: my willing love,
The rather by these arguments of fear,
Set forth in your pursuit.
SEBASTIAN
My kind Antonio,
I can no other answer make but thanks,
And thanks; and ever [ ] oft good turns
Are shuffled off with such uncurrent pay:
But, were my worth as is my conscience firm,
You should find better dealing. What's to do?
Shall we go see the reliques of this town?
ANTONIO
To-morrow, sir: best first go see your lodging.
SEBASTIAN
I am not weary, and 'tis long to night:
I pray you, let us satisfy our eyes
With the memorials and the things of fame
That do renown this city.
ANTONIO
Would you'ld pardon me;
I do not without danger walk these streets:
Once, in a sea-fight, 'gainst the count his galleys
I did some service; of such note indeed,

That were I ta'en here it would scarce be answer'd.

SEBASTIAN

Belike you slew great number of his people.

ANTONIO

The offence is not of such a bloody nature;
Albeit the quality of the time and quarrel
Might well have given us bloody argument.
It might have since been answer'd in repaying
What we took from them; which, for traffic's sake,
Most of our city did: only myself stood out;
For which, if I be lapsed in this place,
I shall pay dear.

SEBASTIAN

Do not then walk too open.

ANTONIO

It doth not fit me. Hold, sir, here's my purse.
In the south suburbs, at the Elephant,
Is best to lodge: I will bespeak our diet,
Whiles you beguile the time and feed your knowledge
With viewing of the town: there shall you have me.

SEBASTIAN

Why I your purse?

ANTONIO

Haply your eye shall light upon some toy
You have desire to purchase; and your store,
I think, is not for idle markets, sir.

SEBASTIAN

I'll be your purse-bearer and leave you
For an hour.

ANTONIO

To the Elephant.

SEBASTIAN

I do remember.

Exeunt

SCENE IV.

OLIVIA's garden.

Enter OLIVIA and MARIA

OLIVIA

I have sent after him: he says he'll come;
How shall I feast him? what bestow of him?
For youth is bought more oft than begg'd or borrow'd.
I speak too loud.
Where is Malvolio? he is sad and civil,
And suits well for a servant with my fortunes:
Where is Malvolio?

MARIA

He's coming, madam; but in very strange manner. He
is, sure, possessed, madam.

OLIVIA

Why, what's the matter? does he rave?

MARIA

No. madam, he does nothing but smile: your
ladyship were best to have some guard about you, if
he come; for, sure, the man is tainted in's wits.

OLIVIA

Go call him hither.

Exit MARIA

I am as mad as he,
If sad and merry madness equal be.

Re-enter MARIA, with MALVOLIO

How now, Malvolio!

MALVOLIO

Sweet lady, ho, ho.

OLIVIA

Smilest thou?
I sent for thee upon a sad occasion.

MALVOLIO

Sad, lady! I could be sad: this does make some
obstruction in the blood, this cross-gartering; but
what of that? if it please the eye of one, it is
with me as the very true sonnet is, 'Please one, and
please all.'

OLIVIA

Why, how dost thou, man? what is the matter with thee?

MALVOLIO

Not black in my mind, though yellow in my legs. It
did come to his hands, and commands shall be
executed: I think we do know the sweet Roman hand.

OLIVIA

Wilt thou go to bed, Malvolio?

MALVOLIO

To bed! ay, sweet-heart, and I'll come to thee.

OLIVIA

God comfort thee! Why dost thou smile so and kiss
thy hand so oft?

MARIA

How do you, Malvolio?

MALVOLIO

At your request! yes; nightingales answer daws.

MARIA

Why appear you with this ridiculous boldness before my lady?

MALVOLIO

'Be not afraid of greatness:' 'twas well writ.

OLIVIA

What meanest thou by that, Malvolio?

MALVOLIO

'Some are born great,'—

OLIVIA

Ha!

MALVOLIO

'Some achieve greatness,'—

OLIVIA

What sayest thou?

MALVOLIO

'And some have greatness thrust upon them.'

OLIVIA

Heaven restore thee!

MALVOLIO

'Remember who commended thy yellow stocking s,'—

OLIVIA

Thy yellow stockings!

MALVOLIO

'And wished to see thee cross-gartered.'

OLIVIA

Cross-gartered!

MALVOLIO

'Go to thou art made, if thou desirest to be so;'—

OLIVIA

Am I made?

MALVOLIO

'If not, let me see thee a servant still.'

OLIVIA

Why, this is very midsummer madness.

Enter Servant

Servant

Madam, the young gentleman of the Count Orsino's is
returned: I could hardly entreat him back: he
attends your ladyship's pleasure.

OLIVIA

I'll come to him.

Exit Servant

Good Maria, let this fellow be looked to. Where's
my cousin Toby? Let some of my people have a special
care of him: I would not have him miscarry for the
half of my dowry.

Exeunt OLIVIA and MARIA

MALVOLIO

O, ho! do you come near me now? no worse man than
Sir Toby to look to me! This concurs directly with
the letter: she sends him on purpose, that I may
appear stubborn to him; for she incites me to that
in the letter. 'Cast thy humble slough,' says she;
'be opposite with a kinsman, surly with servants;
let thy tongue tang with arguments of state; put
thyself into the trick of singularity;' and
consequently sets down the manner how; as, a sad
face, a reverend carriage, a slow tongue, in the
habit of some sir of note, and so forth. I have
limed her; but it is Jove's doing, and Jove make me
thankful! And when she went away now, 'Let this
fellow be looked to:' fellow! not Malvolio, nor
after my degree, but fellow. Why, every thing
adheres together, that no dram of a scruple, no
scruple of a scruple, no obstacle, no incredulous

or unsafe circumstance—What can be said? Nothing
that can be can come between me and the full
prospect of my hopes. Well, Jove, not I, is the
doer of this, and he is to be thanked.

Re-enter MARIA, with SIR TOBY BELCH and FABIAN

SIR TOBY BELCH

Which way is he, in the name of sanctity? If all
the devils of hell be drawn in little, and Legion
himself possessed him, yet I'll speak to him.

FABIAN

Here he is, here he is. How is't with you, sir?
how is't with you, man?

MALVOLIO

Go off; I discard you: let me enjoy my private: go
off.

MARIA

Lo, how hollow the fiend speaks within him! did not
I tell you? Sir Toby, my lady prays you to have a
care of him.

MALVOLIO

Ah, ha! does she so?

SIR TOBY BELCH

Go to, go to; peace, peace; we must deal gently
with him: let me alone. How do you, Malvolio? how
is't with you? What, man! defy the devil:
consider, he's an enemy to mankind.

MALVOLIO

Do you know what you say?

MARIA

La you, an you speak ill of the devil, how he takes
it at heart! Pray God, he be not bewitched!

FABIAN

Carry his water to the wise woman.

MARIA

Marry, and it shall be done to-morrow morning, if I
live. My lady would not lose him for more than I'll say.

MALVOLIO

How now, mistress!

MARIA

O Lord!

SIR TOBY BELCH

Prithee, hold thy peace; this is not the way: do
you not see you move him? let me alone with him.

FABIAN

No way but gentleness; gently, gently: the fiend is
rough, and will not be roughly used.

SIR TOBY BELCH

Why, how now, my bawcock! how dost thou, chuck?

MALVOLIO

Sir!

SIR TOBY BELCH

Ay, Biddy, come with me. What, man! 'tis not for
gravity to play at cherry-pit with Satan: hang
him, foul collier!

MARIA

Get him to say his prayers, good Sir Toby, get him to pray.

MALVOLIO

My prayers, minx!

MARIA

No, I warrant you, he will not hear of godliness.

MALVOLIO

Go, hang yourselves all! you are idle shallow
things: I am not of your element: you shall know
more hereafter.

Exit

SIR TOBY BELCH

Is't possible?

FABIAN

If this were played upon a stage now, I could
condemn it as an improbable fiction.

SIR TOBY BELCH

His very genius hath taken the infection of the device, man.

MARIA

Nay, pursue him now, lest the device take air and taint.

FABIAN

Why, we shall make him mad indeed.

MARIA

The house will be the quieter.

SIR TOBY BELCH

Come, we'll have him in a dark room and bound. My
niece is already in the belief that he's mad: we

may carry it thus, for our pleasure and his penance,
till our very pastime, tired out of breath, prompt
us to have mercy on him: at which time we will
bring the device to the bar and crown thee for a
finder of madmen. But see, but see.

Enter SIR ANDREW

FABIAN

More matter for a May morning.

SIR ANDREW

Here's the challenge, read it: warrant there's
vinegar and pepper in't.

FABIAN

Is't so saucy?

SIR ANDREW

Ay, is't, I warrant him: do but read.

SIR TOBY BELCH

Give me.

Reads

'Youth, whatsoever thou art, thou art but a scurvy fellow.'

FABIAN

Good, and valiant.

SIR TOBY BELCH

[Reads] 'Wonder not, nor admire not in thy mind,
why I do call thee so, for I will show thee no reason for't.'

FABIAN

A good note; that keeps you from the blow of the law.

SIR TOBY BELCH

[Reads] 'Thou comest to the lady Olivia, and in my
sight she uses thee kindly: but thou liest in thy
throat; that is not the matter I challenge thee for.'

FABIAN

Very brief, and to exceeding good sense—less.

SIR TOBY BELCH

[Reads] 'I will waylay thee going home; where if it
be thy chance to kill me,'—

FABIAN

Good.

SIR TOBY BELCH

[Reads] 'Thou killest me like a rogue and a villain.'

FABIAN

Still you keep o' the windy side of the law: good.

SIR TOBY BELCH

[Reads] 'Fare thee well; and God have mercy upon
one of our souls! He may have mercy upon mine; but
my hope is better, and so look to thyself. Thy
friend, as thou usest him, and thy sworn enemy,
ANDREW AGUECHEEK.
If this letter move him not, his legs cannot:
I'll give't him.

MARIA

You may have very fit occasion for't: he is now in
some commerce with my lady, and will by and by depart.

SIR TOBY BELCH

Go, Sir Andrew: scout me for him at the corner the
orchard like a bum-baily: so soon as ever thou seest
him, draw; and, as thou drawest swear horrible; for
it comes to pass oft that a terrible oath, with a
swaggering accent sharply twanged off, gives manhood
more approbation than ever proof itself would have
earned him. Away!

SIR ANDREW

Nay, let me alone for swearing.

Exit

SIR TOBY BELCH

Now will not I deliver his letter: for the behavior
of the young gentleman gives him out to be of good
capacity and breeding; his employment between his
lord and my niece confirms no less: therefore this
letter, being so excellently ignorant, will breed no
terror in the youth: he will find it comes from a
clodpole. But, sir, I will deliver his challenge by
word of mouth; set upon Aguecheek a notable report
of valour; and drive the gentleman, as I know his
youth will aptly receive it, into a most hideous
opinion of his rage, skill, fury and impetuosity.
This will so fright them both that they will kill
one another by the look, like cockatrices.

Re-enter OLIVIA, with VIOLA

FABIAN

Here he comes with your niece: give them way till
he take leave, and presently after him.

SIR TOBY BELCH

I will meditate the while upon some horrid message
for a challenge.

Exeunt SIR TOBY BELCH, FABIAN, and MARIA

OLIVIA

I have said too much unto a heart of stone
And laid mine honour too unchary out:
There's something in me that reproves my fault;
But such a headstrong potent fault it is,
That it but mocks reproof.

VIOLA

With the same 'havior that your passion bears
Goes on my master's grief.

OLIVIA

Here, wear this jewel for me, 'tis my picture;
Refuse it not; it hath no tongue to vex you;
And I beseech you come again to-morrow.
What shall you ask of me that I'll deny,
That honour saved may upon asking give?

VIOLA

Nothing but this; your true love for my master.

OLIVIA

How with mine honour may I give him that
Which I have given to you?

VIOLA

I will acquit you.

OLIVIA

Well, come again to-morrow: fare thee well:
A fiend like thee might bear my soul to hell.

Exit

Re-enter SIR TOBY BELCH and FABIAN

SIR TOBY BELCH

Gentleman, God save thee.

VIOLA

And you, sir.

SIR TOBY BELCH

That defence thou hast, betake thee to't: of what
nature the wrongs are thou hast done him, I know
not; but thy intercepter, full of despite, bloody as
the hunter, attends thee at the orchard-end:
dismount thy tuck, be yare in thy preparation, for

thy assailant is quick, skilful and deadly.

VIOLA

You mistake, sir; I am sure no man hath any quarrel
to me: my remembrance is very free and clear from
any image of offence done to any man.

SIR TOBY BELCH

You'll find it otherwise, I assure you: therefore,
if you hold your life at any price, betake you to
your guard; for your opposite hath in him what
youth, strength, skill and wrath can furnish man withal.

VIOLA

I pray you, sir, what is he?

SIR TOBY BELCH

He is knight, dubbed with unhatched rapier and on
carpet consideration; but he is a devil in private
brawl: souls and bodies hath he divorced three; and
his incensement at this moment is so implacable,
that satisfaction can be none but by pangs of death
and sepulchre. Hob, nob, is his word; give't or take't.

VIOLA

I will return again into the house and desire some
conduct of the lady. I am no fighter. I have heard
of some kind of men that put quarrels purposely on
others, to taste their valour: belike this is a man
of that quirk.

SIR TOBY BELCH

Sir, no; his indignation derives itself out of a
very competent injury: therefore, get you on and
give him his desire. Back you shall not to the
house, unless you undertake that with me which with
as much safety you might answer him: therefore, on,
or strip your sword stark naked; for meddle you
must, that's certain, or forswear to wear iron about you.

VIOLA

This is as uncivil as strange. I beseech you, do me
this courteous office, as to know of the knight what
my offence to him is: it is something of my
negligence, nothing of my purpose.

SIR TOBY BELCH

I will do so. Signior Fabian, stay you by this
gentleman till my return.

Exit

VIOLA

Pray you, sir, do you know of this matter?

FABIAN

I know the knight is incensed against you, even to a
mortal arbitrement; but nothing of the circumstance more.

VIOLA

I beseech you, what manner of man is he?

FABIAN

Nothing of that wonderful promise, to read him by
his form, as you are like to find him in the proof
of his valour. He is, indeed, sir, the most skilful,
bloody and fatal opposite that you could possibly
have found in any part of Illyria. Will you walk
towards him? I will make your peace with him if I
can.

VIOLA

I shall be much bound to you for't: I am one that
had rather go with sir priest than sir knight: I
care not who knows so much of my mettle.

Exeunt

Re-enter SIR TOBY BELCH, with SIR ANDREW

SIR TOBY BELCH

Why, man, he's a very devil; I have not seen such a
firago. I had a pass with him, rapier, scabbard and
all, and he gives me the stuck in with such a mortal
motion, that it is inevitable; and on the answer, he
pays you as surely as your feet hit the ground they
step on. They say he has been fencer to the Sophy.

SIR ANDREW

Pox on't, I'll not meddle with him.

SIR TOBY BELCH

Ay, but he will not now be pacified: Fabian can
scarce hold him yonder.

SIR ANDREW

Plague on't, an I thought he had been valiant and so
cunning in fence, I'ld have seen him damned ere I'ld
have challenged him. Let him let the matter slip,
and I'll give him my horse, grey Capilet.

SIR TOBY BELCH

I'll make the motion: stand here, make a good show

on't: this shall end without the perdition of souls.
Aside
Marry, I'll ride your horse as well as I ride you.
Re-enter FABIAN and VIOLA
To FABIAN
I have his horse to take up the quarrel:
I have persuaded him the youth's a devil.

FABIAN
He is as horribly conceited of him; and pants and
looks pale, as if a bear were at his heels.

SIR TOBY BELCH
[To VIOLA] There's no remedy, sir; he will fight
with you for's oath sake: marry, he hath better
bethought him of his quarrel, and he finds that now
scarce to be worth talking of: therefore draw, for
the supportance of his vow; he protests he will not hurt you.

VIOLA
[Aside] Pray God defend me! A little thing would
make me tell them how much I lack of a man.

FABIAN
Give ground, if you see him furious.

SIR TOBY BELCH
Come, Sir Andrew, there's no remedy; the gentleman
will, for his honour's sake, have one bout with you;
he cannot by the duello avoid it: but he has
promised me, as he is a gentleman and a soldier, he
will not hurt you. Come on; to't.

SIR ANDREW
Pray God, he keep his oath!

VIOLA
I do assure you, 'tis against my will.
They draw
Enter ANTONIO

ANTONIO
Put up your sword. If this young gentleman
Have done offence, I take the fault on me:
If you offend him, I for him defy you.

SIR TOBY BELCH
You, sir! why, what are you?

ANTONIO
One, sir, that for his love dares yet do more

Than you have heard him brag to you he will.

SIR TOBY BELCH

Nay, if you be an undertaker, I am for you.

They draw

Enter Officers

FABIAN

O good Sir Toby, hold! here come the officers.

SIR TOBY BELCH

I'll be with you anon.

VIOLA

Pray, sir, put your sword up, if you please.

SIR ANDREW

Marry, will I, sir; and, for that I promised you,
I'll be as good as my word: he will bear you easily
and reins well.

First Officer

This is the man; do thy office.

Second Officer

Antonio, I arrest thee at the suit of Count Orsino.

ANTONIO

You do mistake me, sir.

First Officer

No, sir, no jot; I know your favour well,
Though now you have no sea-cap on your head.
Take him away: he knows I know him well.

ANTONIO

I must obey.

To VIOLA

This comes with seeking you:
But there's no remedy; I shall answer it.
What will you do, now my necessity
Makes me to ask you for my purse? It grieves me
Much more for what I cannot do for you
Than what befalls myself. You stand amazed;
But be of comfort.

Second Officer

Come, sir, away.

ANTONIO

I must entreat of you some of that money.

VIOLA

What money, sir?

For the fair kindness you have show'd me here,
And, part, being prompted by your present trouble,
Out of my lean and low ability
I'll lend you something: my having is not much;
I'll make division of my present with you:
Hold, there's half my coffer.

ANTONIO

Will you deny me now?
Is't possible that my deserts to you
Can lack persuasion? Do not tempt my misery,
Lest that it make me so unsound a man
As to upbraid you with those kindnesses
That I have done for you.

VIOLA

I know of none;
Nor know I you by voice or any feature:
I hate ingratitude more in a man
Than lying, vainness, babbling, drunkenness,
Or any taint of vice whose strong corruption
Inhabits our frail blood.

ANTONIO

O heavens themselves!

Second Officer

Come, sir, I pray you, go.

ANTONIO

Let me speak a little. This youth that you see here
I snatch'd one half out of the jaws of death,
Relieved him with such sanctity of love,
And to his image, which methought did promise
Most venerable worth, did I devotion.

First Officer

What's that to us? The time goes by: away!

ANTONIO

But O how vile an idol proves this god
Thou hast, Sebastian, done good feature shame.
In nature there's no blemish but the mind;
None can be call'd deform'd but the unkind:
Virtue is beauty, but the beauteous evil
Are empty trunks o'erflourish'd by the devil.

First Officer

The man grows mad: away with him! Come, come, sir.

ANTONIO

Lead me on.

Exit with Officers

VIOLA

Methinks his words do from such passion fly,
That he believes himself: so do not I.
Prove true, imagination, O, prove true,
That I, dear brother, be now ta'en for you!

SIR TOBY BELCH

Come hither, knight; come hither, Fabian: we'll
whisper o'er a couplet or two of most sage saws.

VIOLA

He named Sebastian: I my brother know
Yet living in my glass; even such and so
In favour was my brother, and he went
Still in this fashion, colour, ornament,
For him I imitate: O, if it prove,
Tempests are kind and salt waves fresh in love.

Exit

SIR TOBY BELCH

A very dishonest paltry boy, and more a coward than
a hare: his dishonesty appears in leaving his
friend here in necessity and denying him; and for
his cowardship, ask Fabian.

FABIAN

A coward, a most devout coward, religious in it.

SIR ANDREW

'Slid, I'll after him again and beat him.

SIR TOBY BELCH

Do; cuff him soundly, but never draw thy sword.

SIR ANDREW

An I do not,—

FABIAN

Come, let's see the event.

SIR TOBY BELCH

I dare lay any money 'twill be nothing yet.

Exeunt

Act IV

SCENE I.

Before OLIVIA's house.

Enter SEBASTIAN and Clown

Clown

Will you make me believe that I am not sent for you?

SEBASTIAN

Go to, go to, thou art a foolish fellow:
Let me be clear of thee.

Clown

Well held out, i' faith! No, I do not know you; nor
I am not sent to you by my lady, to bid you come
speak with her; nor your name is not Master Cesario;
nor this is not my nose neither. Nothing that is so is so.

SEBASTIAN

I prithee, vent thy folly somewhere else: Thou
know'st not me.

Clown

Vent my folly! he has heard that word of some
great man and now applies it to a fool. Vent my
folly! I am afraid this great lubber, the world,
will prove a cockney. I prithee now, ungird thy
strangeness and tell me what I shall vent to my
lady: shall I vent to her that thou art coming?

SEBASTIAN

I prithee, foolish Greek, depart from me: There's
money for thee: if you tarry longer, I shall give
worse payment.

Clown

By my troth, thou hast an open hand. These wise men
that give fools money get themselves a good

report—after fourteen years' purchase.

Enter SIR ANDREW, SIR TOBY BELCH, and FABIAN

SIR ANDREW

Now, sir, have I met you again? there's for you.

SEBASTIAN

Why, there's for thee, and there, and there. Are all
the people mad?

SIR TOBY BELCH

Hold, sir, or I'll throw your dagger o'er the house.

Clown

This will I tell my lady straight: I would not be
in some of your coats for two pence.

Exit

SIR TOBY BELCH

Come on, sir; hold.

SIR ANDREW

Nay, let him alone: I'll go another way to work
with him; I'll have an action of battery against
him, if there be any law in Illyria: though I
struck him first, yet it's no matter for that.

SEBASTIAN

Let go thy hand.

SIR TOBY BELCH

Come, sir, I will not let you go. Come, my young
soldier, put up your iron: you are well fleshed; come on.

SEBASTIAN

I will be free from thee. What wouldst thou now? If
thou darest tempt me further, draw thy sword.

SIR TOBY BELCH

What, what? Nay, then I must have an ounce or two
of this malapert blood from you.

Enter OLIVIA

OLIVIA

Hold, Toby; on thy life I charge thee, hold!

SIR TOBY BELCH

Madam!

OLIVIA

Will it be ever thus? Ungracious wretch,
Fit for the mountains and the barbarous caves,
Where manners ne'er were preach'd! out of my sight!
Be not offended, dear Cesario.

Rudesby, be gone!
Exeunt SIR TOBY BELCH, SIR ANDREW, and FABIAN
I prithee, gentle friend,
Let thy fair wisdom, not thy passion, sway
In this uncivil and thou unjust extent
Against thy peace. Go with me to my house,
And hear thou there how many fruitless pranks
This ruffian hath botch'd up, that thou thereby
Mayst smile at this: thou shalt not choose but go:
Do not deny. Beshrew his soul for me,
He started one poor heart of mine in thee.

SEBASTIAN
What relish is in this? how runs the stream?
Or I am mad, or else this is a dream:
Let fancy still my sense in Lethe steep;
If it be thus to dream, still let me sleep!

OLIVIA
Nay, come, I prithee; would thou'ldst be ruled by me!

SEBASTIAN
Madam, I will.

OLIVIA
O, say so, and so be!
Exeunt

SCENE II.

OLIVIA's house.

Enter MARIA and Clown
MARIA
Nay, I prithee, put on this gown and this beard;
make him believe thou art Sir Topas the curate: do
it quickly; I'll call Sir Toby the whilst.
Exit

Clown
Well, I'll put it on, and I will dissemble myself
in't; and I would I were the first that ever
dissembled in such a gown. I am not tall enough to
become the function well, nor lean enough to be

thought a good student; but to be said an honest man
and a good housekeeper goes as fairly as to say a
careful man and a great scholar. The competitors enter.
Enter SIR TOBY BELCH and MARIA

SIR TOBY BELCH

Jove bless thee, master Parson.

Clown

Bonos dies, Sir Toby: for, as the old hermit of
Prague, that never saw pen and ink, very wittily
said to a niece of King Gorboduc, 'That that is is;'
so I, being Master Parson, am Master Parson; for,
what is 'that' but 'that,' and 'is' but 'is'?

SIR TOBY BELCH

To him, Sir Topas.

Clown

What, ho, I say! peace in this prison!

SIR TOBY BELCH

The knave counterfeits well; a good knave.

MALVOLIO

[Within] Who calls there?

Clown

Sir Topas the curate, who comes to visit Malvolio
the lunatic.

MALVOLIO

Sir Topas, Sir Topas, good Sir Topas, go to my lady.

Clown

Out, hyperbolical fiend! how vexest thou this man!
talkest thou nothing but of ladies?

SIR TOBY BELCH

Well said, Master Parson.

MALVOLIO

Sir Topas, never was man thus wronged: good Sir
Topas, do not think I am mad: they have laid me
here in hideous darkness.

Clown

Fie, thou dishonest Satan! I call thee by the most
modest terms; for I am one of those gentle ones
that will use the devil himself with courtesy:
sayest thou that house is dark?

MALVOLIO

As hell, Sir Topas.

Clown

Why it hath bay windows transparent as barricadoes,
and the clearstores toward the south north are as
lustrous as ebony; and yet complainest thou of
obstruction?

MALVOLIO

I am not mad, Sir Topas: I say to you, this house is dark.

Clown

Madman, thou errest: I say, there is no darkness
but ignorance; in which thou art more puzzled than
the Egyptians in their fog.

MALVOLIO

I say, this house is as dark as ignorance, though
ignorance were as dark as hell; and I say, there
was never man thus abused. I am no more mad than you
are: make the trial of it in any constant question.

Clown

What is the opinion of Pythagoras concerning wild fowl?

MALVOLIO

That the soul of our grandam might haply inhabit a bird.

Clown

What thinkest thou of his opinion?

MALVOLIO

I think nobly of the soul, and no way approve his opinion.

Clown

Fare thee well. Remain thou still in darkness:
thou shalt hold the opinion of Pythagoras ere I will
allow of thy wits, and fear to kill a woodcock, lest
thou dispossess the soul of thy grandam. Fare thee well.

MALVOLIO

Sir Topas, Sir Topas!

SIR TOBY BELCH

My most exquisite Sir Topas!

Clown

Nay, I am for all waters.

MARIA

Thou mightst have done this without thy beard and
gown: he sees thee not.

SIR TOBY BELCH

To him in thine own voice, and bring me word how
thou findest him: I would we were well rid of this

knavery. If he may be conveniently delivered, I
would he were, for I am now so far in offence with
my niece that I cannot pursue with any safety this
sport to the upshot. Come by and by to my chamber.
Exeunt SIR TOBY BELCH and MARIA

Clown
[Singing]
'Hey, Robin, jolly Robin,
Tell me how thy lady does.'

MALVOLIO
Fool!

Clown
'My lady is unkind, perdy.'

MALVOLIO
Fool!

Clown
'Alas, why is she so?'

MALVOLIO
Fool, I say!

Clown
'She loves another'—Who calls, ha?

MALVOLIO
Good fool, as ever thou wilt deserve well at my
hand, help me to a candle, and pen, ink and paper:
as I am a gentleman, I will live to be thankful to
thee for't.

Clown
Master Malvolio?

MALVOLIO
Ay, good fool.

Clown
Alas, sir, how fell you besides your five wits?

MALVOLIO
Fool, there was never a man so notoriously abused: I
am as well in my wits, fool, as thou art.

Clown
But as well? then you are mad indeed, if you be no
better in your wits than a fool.

MALVOLIO
They have here propertied me; keep me in darkness,
send ministers to me, asses, and do all they can to

face me out of my wits.

Clown

Advise you what you say; the minister is here.
Malvolio, Malvolio, thy wits the heavens restore!
endeavour thyself to sleep, and leave thy vain
bibble babble.

MALVOLIO

Sir Topas!

Clown

Maintain no words with him, good fellow. Who, I,
sir? not I, sir. God be wi' you, good Sir Topas.
Merry, amen. I will, sir, I will.

MALVOLIO

Fool, fool, fool, I say!

Clown

Alas, sir, be patient. What say you sir? I am
shent for speaking to you.

MALVOLIO

Good fool, help me to some light and some paper: I
tell thee, I am as well in my wits as any man in Illyria.

Clown

Well-a-day that you were, sir

MALVOLIO

By this hand, I am. Good fool, some ink, paper and
light; and convey what I will set down to my lady:
it shall advantage thee more than ever the bearing
of letter did.

Clown

I will help you to't. But tell me true, are you
not mad indeed? or do you but counterfeit?

MALVOLIO

Believe me, I am not; I tell thee true.

Clown

Nay, I'll ne'er believe a madman till I see his
brains. I will fetch you light and paper and ink.

MALVOLIO

Fool, I'll requite it in the highest degree: I
prithee, be gone.

Clown

[Singing]
I am gone, sir,

And anon, sir,
I'll be with you again,
In a trice,
Like to the old Vice,
Your need to sustain;
Who, with dagger of lath,
In his rage and his wrath,
Cries, ah, ha! to the devil:
Like a mad lad,
Pare thy nails, dad;
Adieu, good man devil.
Exit

SCENE III.

OLIVIA's garden.

Enter SEBASTIAN
SEBASTIAN
This is the air; that is the glorious sun;
This pearl she gave me, I do feel't and see't;
And though 'tis wonder that enwraps me thus,
Yet 'tis not madness. Where's Antonio, then?
I could not find him at the Elephant:
Yet there he was; and there I found this credit,
That he did range the town to seek me out.
His counsel now might do me golden service;
For though my soul disputes well with my sense,
That this may be some error, but no madness,
Yet doth this accident and flood of fortune
So far exceed all instance, all discourse,
That I am ready to distrust mine eyes
And wrangle with my reason that persuades me
To any other trust but that I am mad
Or else the lady's mad; yet, if 'twere so,
She could not sway her house, command her followers,
Take and give back affairs and their dispatch
With such a smooth, discreet and stable bearing
As I perceive she does: there's something in't

That is deceiveable. But here the lady comes.
Enter OLIVIA and Priest
OLIVIA
Blame not this haste of mine. If you mean well,
Now go with me and with this holy man
Into the chantry by: there, before him,
And underneath that consecrated roof,
Plight me the full assurance of your faith;
That my most jealous and too doubtful soul
May live at peace. He shall conceal it
Whiles you are willing it shall come to note,
What time we will our celebration keep
According to my birth. What do you say?
SEBASTIAN
I'll follow this good man, and go with you;
And, having sworn truth, ever will be true.
OLIVIA
Then lead the way, good father; and heavens so shine,
That they may fairly note this act of mine!
Exeunt

Act V

SCENE I.

Before OLIVIA's house.

Enter Clown and FABIAN

FABIAN

Now, as thou lovest me, let me see his letter.

Clown

Good Master Fabian, grant me another request.

FABIAN

Any thing.

Clown

Do not desire to see this letter.

FABIAN

This is, to give a dog, and in recompense desire my
dog again.

Enter DUKE ORSINO, VIOLA, CURIO, and Lords

DUKE ORSINO

Belong you to the Lady Olivia, friends?

Clown

Ay, sir; we are some of her trappings.

DUKE ORSINO

I know thee well; how dost thou, my good fellow?

Clown

Truly, sir, the better for my foes and the worse
for my friends.

DUKE ORSINO

Just the contrary; the better for thy friends.

Clown

No, sir, the worse.

DUKE ORSINO

How can that be?

Clown

Marry, sir, they praise me and make an ass of me;
now my foes tell me plainly I am an ass: so that by
my foes, sir I profit in the knowledge of myself,
and by my friends, I am abused: so that,
conclusions to be as kisses, if your four negatives
make your two affirmatives why then, the worse for
my friends and the better for my foes.

DUKE ORSINO

Why, this is excellent.

Clown

By my troth, sir, no; though it please you to be
one of my friends.

DUKE ORSINO

Thou shalt not be the worse for me: there's gold.

Clown

But that it would be double-dealing, sir, I would
you could make it another.

DUKE ORSINO

O, you give me ill counsel.

Clown

Put your grace in your pocket, sir, for this once,
and let your flesh and blood obey it.

DUKE ORSINO

Well, I will be so much a sinner, to be a
double-dealer: there's another.

Clown

Primo, secundo, tertio, is a good play; and the old
saying is, the third pays for all: the triplex,
sir, is a good tripping measure; or the bells of
Saint Bennet, sir, may put you in mind; one, two, three.

DUKE ORSINO

You can fool no more money out of me at this throw:
if you will let your lady know I am here to speak
with her, and bring her along with you, it may awake
my bounty further.

Clown

Marry, sir, lullaby to your bounty till I come
again. I go, sir; but I would not have you to think
that my desire of having is the sin of covetousness:
but, as you say, sir, let your bounty take a nap, I

will awake it anon.

Exit

VIOLA

Here comes the man, sir, that did rescue me.

Enter ANTONIO and Officers

DUKE ORSINO

That face of his I do remember well;

Yet, when I saw it last, it was besmear'd

As black as Vulcan in the smoke of war:

A bawbling vessel was he captain of,

For shallow draught and bulk unprizable;

With which such scathful grapple did he make

With the most noble bottom of our fleet,

That very envy and the tongue of loss

Cried fame and honour on him. What's the matter?

First Officer

Orsino, this is that Antonio

That took the Phoenix and her fraught from Candy;

And this is he that did the Tiger board,

When your young nephew Titus lost his leg:

Here in the streets, desperate of shame and state,

In private brabble did we apprehend him.

VIOLA

He did me kindness, sir, drew on my side;

But in conclusion put strange speech upon me:

I know not what 'twas but distraction.

DUKE ORSINO

Notable pirate! thou salt-water thief!

What foolish boldness brought thee to their mercies,

Whom thou, in terms so bloody and so dear,

Hast made thine enemies?

ANTONIO

Orsino, noble sir,

Be pleased that I shake off these names you give me:

Antonio never yet was thief or pirate,

Though I confess, on base and ground enough,

Orsino's enemy. A witchcraft drew me hither:

That most ingrateful boy there by your side,

From the rude sea's enraged and foamy mouth

Did I redeem; a wreck past hope he was:

His life I gave him and did thereto add

My love, without retention or restraint,
All his in dedication; for his sake
Did I expose myself, pure for his love,
Into the danger of this adverse town;
Drew to defend him when he was beset:
Where being apprehended, his false cunning,
Not meaning to partake with me in danger,
Taught him to face me out of his acquaintance,
And grew a twenty years removed thing
While one would wink; denied me mine own purse,
Which I had recommended to his use
Not half an hour before.

VIOLA

How can this be?

DUKE ORSINO

When came he to this town?

ANTONIO

To-day, my lord; and for three months before,
No interim, not a minute's vacancy,
Both day and night did we keep company.

Enter OLIVIA and Attendants

DUKE ORSINO

Here comes the countess: now heaven walks on earth.
But for thee, fellow; fellow, thy words are madness:
Three months this youth hath tended upon me;
But more of that anon. Take him aside.

OLIVIA

What would my lord, but that he may not have,
Wherein Olivia may seem serviceable?
Cesario, you do not keep promise with me.

VIOLA

Madam!

DUKE ORSINO

Gracious Olivia,—

OLIVIA

What do you say, Cesario? Good my lord,—

VIOLA

My lord would speak; my duty hushes me.

OLIVIA

If it be aught to the old tune, my lord,
It is as fat and fulsome to mine ear

As howling after music.

DUKE ORSINO

Still so cruel?

OLIVIA

Still so constant, lord.

DUKE ORSINO

What, to perverseness? you uncivil lady,
To whose ingrate and unauspicious altars
My soul the faithfull'st offerings hath breathed out
That e'er devotion tender'd! What shall I do?

OLIVIA

Even what it please my lord, that shall become him.

DUKE ORSINO

Why should I not, had I the heart to do it,
Like to the Egyptian thief at point of death,
Kill what I love?—a savage jealousy
That sometimes savours nobly. But hear me this:
Since you to non-regardance cast my faith,
And that I partly know the instrument
That screws me from my true place in your favour,
Live you the marble-breasted tyrant still;
But this your minion, whom I know you love,
And whom, by heaven I swear, I tender dearly,
Him will I tear out of that cruel eye,
Where he sits crowned in his master's spite.
Come, boy, with me; my thoughts are ripe in mischief:
I'll sacrifice the lamb that I do love,
To spite a raven's heart within a dove.

VIOLA

And I, most jocund, apt and willingly,
To do you rest, a thousand deaths would die.

OLIVIA

Where goes Cesario?

VIOLA

After him I love
More than I love these eyes, more than my life,
More, by all mores, than e'er I shall love wife.
If I do feign, you witnesses above
Punish my life for tainting of my love!

OLIVIA

Ay me, detested! how am I beguiled!

VIOLA

Who does beguile you? who does do you wrong?

OLIVIA

Hast thou forgot thyself? is it so long?
Call forth the holy father.

DUKE ORSINO

Come, away!

OLIVIA

Whither, my lord? Cesario, husband, stay.

DUKE ORSINO

Husband!

OLIVIA

Ay, husband: can he that deny?

DUKE ORSINO

Her husband, sirrah!

VIOLA

No, my lord, not I.

OLIVIA

Alas, it is the baseness of thy fear
That makes thee strangle thy propriety:
Fear not, Cesario; take thy fortunes up;
Be that thou know'st thou art, and then thou art
As great as that thou fear'st.

Enter Priest

O, welcome, father!
Father, I charge thee, by thy reverence,
Here to unfold, though lately we intended
To keep in darkness what occasion now
Reveals before 'tis ripe, what thou dost know
Hath newly pass'd between this youth and me.

Priest

A contract of eternal bond of love,
Confirm'd by mutual joinder of your hands,
Attested by the holy close of lips,
Strengthen'd by interchangement of your rings;
And all the ceremony of this compact
Seal'd in my function, by my testimony:
Since when, my watch hath told me, toward my grave
I have travell'd but two hours.

DUKE ORSINO

O thou dissembling cub! what wilt thou be

When time hath sow'd a grizzle on thy case?
Or will not else thy craft so quickly grow,
That thine own trip shall be thine overthrow?
Farewell, and take her; but direct thy feet
Where thou and I henceforth may never meet.

VIOLA

My lord, I do protest—

OLIVIA

O, do not swear!
Hold little faith, though thou hast too much fear.

Enter SIR ANDREW

SIR ANDREW

For the love of God, a surgeon! Send one presently
to Sir Toby.

OLIVIA

What's the matter?

SIR ANDREW

He has broke my head across and has given Sir Toby
a bloody coxcomb too: for the love of God, your
help! I had rather than forty pound I were at home.

OLIVIA

Who has done this, Sir Andrew?

SIR ANDREW

The count's gentleman, one Cesario: we took him for
a coward, but he's the very devil incardinate.

DUKE ORSINO

My gentleman, Cesario?

SIR ANDREW

'Od's lifelings, here he is! You broke my head for
nothing; and that that I did, I was set on to do't
by Sir Toby.

VIOLA

Why do you speak to me? I never hurt you:
You drew your sword upon me without cause;
But I bespoke you fair, and hurt you not.

SIR ANDREW

If a bloody coxcomb be a hurt, you have hurt me: I
think you set nothing by a bloody coxcomb.

Enter SIR TOBY BELCH and Clown

Here comes Sir Toby halting; you shall hear more:
but if he had not been in drink, he would have

tickled you othergates than he did.

DUKE ORSINO

How now, gentleman! how is't with you?

SIR TOBY BELCH

That's all one: has hurt me, and there's the end
on't. Sot, didst see Dick surgeon, sot?

Clown

O, he's drunk, Sir Toby, an hour agone; his eyes
were set at eight i' the morning.

SIR TOBY BELCH

Then he's a rogue, and a passy measures panyn: I
hate a drunken rogue.

OLIVIA

Away with him! Who hath made this havoc with them?

SIR ANDREW

I'll help you, Sir Toby, because well be dressed together.

SIR TOBY BELCH

Will you help? an ass-head and a coxcomb and a
knave, a thin-faced knave, a gull!

OLIVIA

Get him to bed, and let his hurt be look'd to.

Exeunt Clown, FABIAN, SIR TOBY BELCH, and SIR ANDREW
Enter SEBASTIAN

SEBASTIAN

I am sorry, madam, I have hurt your kinsman:
But, had it been the brother of my blood,
I must have done no less with wit and safety.
You throw a strange regard upon me, and by that
I do perceive it hath offended you:
Pardon me, sweet one, even for the vows
We made each other but so late ago.

DUKE ORSINO

One face, one voice, one habit, and two persons,
A natural perspective, that is and is not!

SEBASTIAN

Antonio, O my dear Antonio!
How have the hours rack'd and tortured me,
Since I have lost thee!

ANTONIO

Sebastian are you?

SEBASTIAN
Fear'st thou that, Antonio?

ANTONIO
How have you made division of yourself?
An apple, cleft in two, is not more twin
Than these two creatures. Which is Sebastian?

OLIVIA
Most wonderful!

SEBASTIAN
Do I stand there? I never had a brother;
Nor can there be that deity in my nature,
Of here and every where. I had a sister,
Whom the blind waves and surges have devour'd.
Of charity, what kin are you to me?
What countryman? what name? what parentage?

VIOLA
Of Messaline: Sebastian was my father;
Such a Sebastian was my brother too,
So went he suited to his watery tomb:
If spirits can assume both form and suit
You come to fright us.

SEBASTIAN
A spirit I am indeed;
But am in that dimension grossly clad
Which from the womb I did participate.
Were you a woman, as the rest goes even,
I should my tears let fall upon your cheek,
And say 'Thrice-welcome, drowned Viola!'

VIOLA
My father had a mole upon his brow.

SEBASTIAN
And so had mine.

VIOLA
And died that day when Viola from her birth
Had number'd thirteen years.

SEBASTIAN
O, that record is lively in my soul!
He finished indeed his mortal act
That day that made my sister thirteen years.

VIOLA
If nothing lets to make us happy both

But this my masculine usurp'd attire,
Do not embrace me till each circumstance
Of place, time, fortune, do cohere and jump
That I am Viola: which to confirm,
I'll bring you to a captain in this town,
Where lie my maiden weeds; by whose gentle help
I was preserved to serve this noble count.
All the occurrence of my fortune since
Hath been between this lady and this lord.

SEBASTIAN

[To OLIVIA] So comes it, lady, you have been mistook:
But nature to her bias drew in that.
You would have been contracted to a maid;
Nor are you therein, by my life, deceived,
You are betroth'd both to a maid and man.

DUKE ORSINO

Be not amazed; right noble is his blood.
If this be so, as yet the glass seems true,
I shall have share in this most happy wreck.

To VIOLA

Boy, thou hast said to me a thousand times
Thou never shouldst love woman like to me.

VIOLA

And all those sayings will I overswear;
And those swearings keep as true in soul
As doth that orbed continent the fire
That severs day from night.

DUKE ORSINO

Give me thy hand;
And let me see thee in thy woman's weeds.

VIOLA

The captain that did bring me first on shore
Hath my maid's garments: he upon some action
Is now in durance, at Malvolio's suit,
A gentleman, and follower of my lady's.

OLIVIA

He shall enlarge him: fetch Malvolio hither:
And yet, alas, now I remember me,
They say, poor gentleman, he's much distract.
Re-enter Clown with a letter, and FABIAN
A most extracting frenzy of mine own

From my remembrance clearly banish'd his.
How does he, sirrah?

Clown

Truly, madam, he holds Belzebub at the staves's end as
well as a man in his case may do: has here writ a
letter to you; I should have given't you to-day
morning, but as a madman's epistles are no gospels,
so it skills not much when they are delivered.

OLIVIA

Open't, and read it.

Clown

Look then to be well edified when the fool delivers
the madman.

Reads

'By the Lord, madam,'—

OLIVIA

How now! art thou mad?

Clown

No, madam, I do but read madness: an your ladyship
will have it as it ought to be, you must allow Vox.

OLIVIA

Prithee, read i' thy right wits.

Clown

So I do, madonna; but to read his right wits is to
read thus: therefore perpend, my princess, and give ear.

OLIVIA

Read it you, sirrah.

To FABIAN

FABIAN

[Reads] 'By the Lord, madam, you wrong me, and the
world shall know it: though you have put me into
darkness and given your drunken cousin rule over
me, yet have I the benefit of my senses as well as
your ladyship. I have your own letter that induced
me to the semblance I put on; with the which I doubt
not but to do myself much right, or you much shame.
Think of me as you please. I leave my duty a little
unthought of and speak out of my injury.
THE MADLY-USED MALVOLIO.'

OLIVIA

Did he write this?

Clown
Ay, madam.
DUKE ORSINO
This savours not much of distraction.
OLIVIA
See him deliver'd, Fabian; bring him hither.
Exit FABIAN
My lord so please you, these things further
thought on,
To think me as well a sister as a wife,
One day shall crown the alliance on't, so please you,
Here at my house and at my proper cost.
DUKE ORSINO
Madam, I am most apt to embrace your offer.
To VIOLA
Your master quits you; and for your service done him,
So much against the mettle of your sex,
So far beneath your soft and tender breeding,
And since you call'd me master for so long,
Here is my hand: you shall from this time be
Your master's mistress.
OLIVIA
A sister! you are she.
Re-enter FABIAN, with MALVOLIO
DUKE ORSINO
Is this the madman?
OLIVIA
Ay, my lord, this same.
How now, Malvolio!
MALVOLIO
Madam, you have done me wrong,
Notorious wrong.
OLIVIA
Have I, Malvolio? no.
MALVOLIO
Lady, you have. Pray you, peruse that letter.
You must not now deny it is your hand:
Write from it, if you can, in hand or phrase;
Or say 'tis not your seal, nor your invention:
You can say none of this: well, grant it then
And tell me, in the modesty of honour,

Why you have given me such clear lights of favour,
Bade me come smiling and cross-garter'd to you,
To put on yellow stockings and to frown
Upon Sir Toby and the lighter people;
And, acting this in an obedient hope,
Why have you suffer'd me to be imprison'd,
Kept in a dark house, visited by the priest,
And made the most notorious geck and gull
That e'er invention play'd on? tell me why.

OLIVIA
Alas, Malvolio, this is not my writing,
Though, I confess, much like the character
But out of question 'tis Maria's hand.
And now I do bethink me, it was she
First told me thou wast mad; then camest in smiling,
And in such forms which here were presupposed
Upon thee in the letter. Prithee, be content:
This practise hath most shrewdly pass'd upon thee;
But when we know the grounds and authors of it,
Thou shalt be both the plaintiff and the judge
Of thine own cause.

FABIAN
Good madam, hear me speak,
And let no quarrel nor no brawl to come
Taint the condition of this present hour,
Which I have wonder'd at. In hope it shall not,
Most freely I confess, myself and Toby
Set this device against Malvolio here,
Upon some stubborn and uncourteous parts
We had conceived against him: Maria writ
The letter at Sir Toby's great importance;
In recompense whereof he hath married her.
How with a sportful malice it was follow'd,
May rather pluck on laughter than revenge;
If that the injuries be justly weigh'd
That have on both sides pass'd.

OLIVIA
Alas, poor fool, how have they baffled thee!

Clown
Why, 'some are born great, some achieve greatness,
and some have greatness thrown upon them.' I was

one, sir, in this interlude; one Sir Topas, sir; but
that's all one. 'By the Lord, fool, I am not mad.'
But do you remember? 'Madam, why laugh you at such
a barren rascal? an you smile not, he's gagged:'
and thus the whirligig of time brings in his revenges.

MALVOLIO

I'll be revenged on the whole pack of you.

Exit

OLIVIA

He hath been most notoriously abused.

DUKE ORSINO

Pursue him and entreat him to a peace:
He hath not told us of the captain yet:
When that is known and golden time convents,
A solemn combination shall be made
Of our dear souls. Meantime, sweet sister,
We will not part from hence. Cesario, come;
For so you shall be, while you are a man;
But when in other habits you are seen,
Orsino's mistress and his fancy's queen.

Exeunt all, except Clown

Clown

[Sings]
When that I was and a little tiny boy,
With hey, ho, the wind and the rain,
A foolish thing was but a toy,
For the rain it raineth every day.
But when I came to man's estate,
With hey, ho, & c.
'Gainst knaves and thieves men shut their gate,
For the rain, & c.
But when I came, alas! to wive,
With hey, ho, & c.
By swaggering could I never thrive,
For the rain, & c.
But when I came unto my beds,
With hey, ho, & c.
With toss-pots still had drunken heads,
For the rain, & c.
A great while ago the world begun,
With hey, ho, & c.

But that's all one, our play is done,
And we'll strive to please you every day.
Exit

Made in the USA
Lexington, KY
20 August 2019